WHAT IS REAL?

Space-Time Singularities or Quantum Black Holes? Dark Matter or Planck Mass Particles? General Relativity or Quantum Gravity? Volume or Area Entropy Law?

BALUNGI FRANCIS

Copyright © BalungiFrancis, 2020

The moral right of the author has been asserted.

All rights reserved. Apart from any fair dealing for the purposes of research or private study or critism or review, no part of this publication may be reproduced, distributed, or transmitted in any form or by any means, including photocopying, recording, or other electronic or mechanical methods, or by any information storage and retrieval system without the prior written permission of the publisher.

TABLE OF CONTENTS

DEDICATION   *1*

PREFACE   *ii*

Space-time Singularity or Quantum Black Holes?
1

What is real? Is it Volume or Area Entropy Law of Black Holes?   *8*

Is it Dark Matter, MOND or Quantum Black Holes? 12

What is real? General Relativity or Quantum Gravity
20

Particle Creation by Black Holes: Is it Hawking's Approach or My Approach?   *28*

Stellar Mass Black Holes or Primordial Holes 39

Additional Readings   *43*

Hidden in Plain sight1: A Simple Link between Quantum Mechanics and Relativity   44

Hidden in Plain sight2: From White Dwarfs to Black Holes   50

Appendix 1   63

Derivation of the Energy density stored in the Electric field and Gravitational Field   63

Epilogue   65

Glossary   67

Bibliography   83

Acknowledgments   94

DEDICATION

To Carlo Rovelli

PREFACE

What exactly is physical reality? In elegant and accessible prose, theoretical physicist Balungi Francis leads us on a wondrous journey from space-time singularities to Quantum Black Holes without information loss, from the Bekenstein-Hawking Area entropy law to his famous Volume entropy law of Black holes, from Modified Newtonian Dynamics, Dark Matter to Planck mass particles, from White Dwarfs to Black Holes and from General Relativity to his own work in Quantum Gravity. As he shows us how the idea of reality has evolved overtime, Balungi offers deeper explanations of the theories he introduced so concisely in Quantum Gravity in a Nutshell1. Balungi invites us to imagine a marvelous world where space breaks up into tiny grains, singularities disappears, information loss in BHs resolved, time disappears at the smallest scales, and black holes are waiting to explode.

    This wonderful and exciting book is optimal for physics graduate students and researchers. The physical explanations are exceedingly well written and integrated with formulas. Quantum Gravity is the next big thing and this book will help the reader understand and use the theory.

Balungi Francis 2020

Space-time Singularity or Quantum Black Holes?

It has been known for some time that a star more than three times the size of our Sun collapses in this way, the gravitational forces of the entire mass of a star overcomes the electromagnetic forces of individual atoms and so collapse inwards. If a star is massive enough it will continue to collapse creating a Black hole, where the whopping of space time is so great that nothing can escape not even light, it gets smaller and smaller. The star in fact gets denser as atoms even subatomic particles literally get crashed into smaller and smaller space, and its ending point is of course a space time singularity.

In summary, a Black hole is that object created when a dying star collapses to a singular point, concealed by an event horizon, it is so dense and has strong gravity that nothing, including light, can escape it. Black holes are predicted by general relativity, and though they cannot be "seen," several have been inferred from astronomical observations of binary stars and massive collapsed stars at the centers of galaxies.

Black holes formed by gravitational collapse require great energy density but there exists a new breed of Black holes that where formed in the early universe after the big bang, where the energy density was much greater allowing the formation of Primordial Black holes with masses ranging from, $10^8, 10^{12} - 10^{17} kg$. Therefore the formation of primordial, min or quantum black holes was due to density perturbations forming in it a gravitational collapse in the early universe.

A Black hole might not actually be a physical object in space but rather a mathematical singularity, a prediction of Einstein's General Relativity theory, a place where the solutions of Einstein differential equations break down. A space-time singularity therefore is a position in space where quantities used to determine the gravitational field become infinite; such quantities include the curvature of space-time and the density of matter. Singularities are places where both the curvature and the energy-density of matter become infinitely large such that light cannot escape them. This happens for example inside black holes and at the beginning of the early universe.

Singularities in any physical theory indicate that either something is wrong or we need to reformulate the theory itself. Singularities are like dividing something by zero. The problems in General relativity arise from trying to deal with a point in space or a universe that is zero in size (infinite densities). However, quantum mechanics suggests that there may be no such thing in nature as a point in space-time, implying that space-time is always smeared out, occupying some minimum region. The minimum smeared-out volume of space-time is a profound property in any quantized theory of gravity and such an outcome lies in a widespread expectation that singularities will be resolved in a quantum theory of gravity. This implies that the study of singularities acts as a testing ground for quantum gravity.

Loop quantum gravity (LQG) suggests that singularities may not exist. LQG states that due to quantum gravity effects, there must be a minimum distance beyond which the force of gravity no longer continues to increase as the distance between the masses become shorter or alternatively that interpenetrating particle waves mask gravitational effects that would be felt at a distance. It must also be true that under the assumption of a corrected dynamical equation of LQ cosmology and brane world model, for the gravitational collapse of a perfect fluid sphere in the commoving frame, the sphere does not collapse to a singularity but instead pulsates between a maximum and minimum size, avoiding the singularity.

Additionally, the information loss paradox is also a hot topic of theoretical modeling right now because it suggests that either our theory of quantum physics or our model of black holes is flawed or at least incomplete. and perhaps most importantly, it is also recognized with some prescience that resolving the information paradox will hold the key to a holistic description of quantum gravity, and therefore be a major advance towards a unified field theory of physics.

Singularities are a sign that the theory breaks down and has to be replaced by a more fundamental theory. And we think the same has to be the case in General Relativity, where the more fundamental theory to replace it is quantum gravity.

If black holes are as a result of the solutions to the Einstein's differential equations breaking down, then what is real?

Whether in gravitational collapse or the early universe, we now know that the formation of Black holes or space time singularities requires great and much greater energy density. This we know because while the left hand side of Einstein field equations representsnts the metric of space-time curvature, the right hand side represents the matter- energy content of the classical matter fields of pressure and energy density. This therefore means that quantum mechanics which plays an important role in the behavior of the matter fields has no place in the Einstein field equations and this is what brings on the singularities that plague the general relativity theory.

$$G_{\mu\nu} + \Lambda g_{\mu\nu} = \frac{8\pi G}{c^4} T_{\mu\nu}$$

Because of this, one therefore has a problem of defining a consistent scheme in which the space time metric is treated classically but is coupled to the matter fields which are treated quantum mechanically.

What is not real is to use the stress energy tensor (classical pressure and energy density) on Black holes instead of the quantum mechanical energy density.

The approximation I shall use on my journey to quantum gravity (Quantum Black holes) is that the matter fields, such as scalar, electro-magnetic, or neutrino fields, obey the usual wave equations with the left hand side replaced by a classical space time second order curvature ($\Lambda = \frac{1}{R^2}$), where R is the radius of curvature) while the right hand stress-energy tensor replaced by the quantum mechanical energy density ($\rho = \frac{F^2}{8\pi\alpha\hbar c}$ (1)) Where F is the force involved in an interaction α is the coupling constant that determines the strength of the force, and ℏ is the reduced Planck constant. The equation represents the coupling constant (α) as a function of the energy density (ρ) for any force (F) exerted in an interaction. The application of this equation is the Franzl Aus Tirol curve on Wikipedia's "Coupling constant". Another application is the derivation of energy stored in the electromagnetic field (see Appendix 1).Therefore the general theory of quantum mechanics in curved space –time will be given by this simple equation, $\Lambda = \frac{8\pi G}{c^4}\rho$, where

$$\Lambda = \frac{GF^2}{\alpha\hbar c^5} = \frac{F^2}{\alpha E_{pl}^2} \qquad (2)$$

Where, $E_{pl} = M_{pl}c^2$ is the Planck energy and M_{pl} is the Planck mass

From the above given equation we see that high space curvature will always be achieved when the square of the force involved increases. According to the theory given, this will only occur at the Planck energy level where space is discrete or granular in nature (its building blocks being exactly the Planck mass, simply put, the atoms of space). There is no change in energy because the only energy involved in the process is the constant Planck energy of the Planck mass.

As we said earlier, that the formation of a black hole due to the process of gravitational collapse occurs in the presence of great energy density and also that the formation of primordial black holes in the early universe occurs in the presence of a much greater energy density, our theory suggests that this energy density is high because of the strong gravitational force involved in the process. According to general relativity, this force is a constant and is given by, $F = \frac{c^4}{G}$. Therefore from equation (2), when this force is present the curvature of space scales as the inverse of the square of the Planck length,

$$\Lambda = \frac{c^3}{\alpha \hbar G} = \frac{1}{\alpha l_p{}^2} \qquad (3)$$

Where $l_p = \sqrt{\frac{\hbar G}{c^3}}$ is the Planck length.

This implies that, in the theory of quantum mechanics in curved space-time for the gravitational collapse of a star, the star does not collapse to a singularity but instead to a Planck sized star of Planck length close to $10^{-35} m$ and this will happen only when $\alpha = 1$. Finally, in the theory of quantum mechanics in curved space-time, we consider the possibility that the energy of a collapsing star and any additional energy falling into the hole could condense into a highly compressed core with density of the order of the Planck density. Since the energy density or pressure is expressed as in equation (1),

$$\rho = \frac{F^2}{8\pi \alpha \hbar c}$$

Therefore nature appears to enter the quantum gravity regime when the energy density of matter reaches the Planck scale. The point is that this may happen well before relevant lengths become planckian. For instance, a collapsing spatially compact universe bounces back into an expanding one. The bounce is due to a quantum-gravitational repulsion which originates from the modified Heisenberg uncertainty, and is akin to the force that keeps an electron from falling into the nucleus. And from the uncertainity principle, this repulsion force is given by,

$$F = \frac{c^4}{G}$$

Therefore the bounce does not happen when the universe is of planckian size, as before; it happens when the matter energy density reaches the Planck density in this way,

$$\rho = \frac{c^7}{8\pi\alpha\hbar G^2} \qquad (4)$$

At this energy density, a Planck star is formed. The key feature of this theoretical object is that this repulsion arises from the energy density, not the Planck length, and starts taking effect far earlier than might be expected. This repulsive 'force' is strong enough to stop the collapse of the star well before a singularity is formed, and indeed, well before the Planck scale for distance. Since a Planck star is calculated to be considerably larger than the Planck scale for distance, this means there is adequate room for all the information captured inside of a black hole to be encoded in the star, thus avoiding information loss.

The analogy between quantum gravitational effects on Cosmological and black-hole singularities has been exploited to study if and how quantum gravity could also resolve the $r = 0$ singularity at the center of a collapsed star, and there are good indications that it does. For example, if we extend (3) to n extra dimensions we have,

$$R = \alpha^{n/2} l_p$$

Where α in this case is the size of the extra dimensions and α^n is the flux in the extra dimesions. Let the size of the extra dimension be given as the gravitational coupling constant, $\alpha = \frac{GM^2}{\hbar c} = \left(\frac{M}{M_{pl}}\right)^2$, then the size of a star will be given by,

$$r = \left(\frac{M}{M_{pl}}\right)^n l_p \quad (5)$$

Where M is the mass of the star and n is positive. For instance, if $n = 1/3$, a stellar-mass black hole would collapse to a Planck star with a size of the order of 10^{-10} centimeters. This is very small compared to the original star in fact, smaller than the atomic scale but it is still more than 30 orders of magnitude larger than the Planck length. This is the scale on which we are focusing here. The main hypothesis here is that a star so compressed would not satisfy the classical Einstein equations anymore, even if huge compared to the Planck scale. Because its energy density is already planckian.

What is real is that; the gravitational collapse of a star does not lead to a singularity but to one additional phase in the life of a star: a quantum gravitational phase where the gravitational attraction is balanced by a quantum pressure.

What is real? Is it Volume or Area Entropy Law of Black Holes?

The development of general relativity followed a publication of acceleration under special relativity in 1907 by Albert Einstein. In his article, he argued that any mass will "Distort" the region of space around it so that all freely moving objects will follow the same curved paths curving toward the mass producing the distortions. Then in 1916, Schwarzschild found a solution to the Einstein field equations, laying the groundwork for the description of gravitational collapse and eventually black holes.

A black hole is created when a dying star collapses to a singular point, concealed by an "event horizon;" the black hole is so dense and has such strong gravity that nothing, including light, can escape it; black holes are predicted by general relativity, and though they cannot be "seen," several have been inferred from astronomical observations of binary stars and massive collapsed stars at the centers of galaxies.

These objects have puzzled the minds of great thinkers for many years. History puts it that, they were first predicated by John Michell and Pierre-Simon Laplace in the 18th century but David Finkelstein was the first person to publish a promising explanation of them in 1958 based on Karl Schwarz child's formulations of a solution to general relativity that characterized black holes in 1916.

In 1971, Hawking developed what is known as the second law of black hole mechanics in which the total area of the event horizons of any collection of classical black holes can never decrease, even if they collide and merge. This was similar to the second law of thermodynamics which states that, the entropy of a system can never decrease.

Then in 1972 Bekenstein proposed an analogy between black hole physics and thermodynamics in which he derived a relation between the entropy of black hole entropy and the area of its event horizon.

$$S = \frac{Akc^3}{4G\hbar}$$

In 1974, Hawking predicted an entirely astonishing phenomenon about black holes, in which he ascertained with accuracy that black holes do radiate or emit particles in a perfect black body spectrum.

$$T = \frac{\hbar c^3}{8\pi GMk}$$

The Bekenstein-Hawking area entropy law raises a number of questions. Why does the entropy of a Black hole scale with its area and not with its volume? For systems that we have studied, the entropy is proportional to the volume of the system. If entropy is proportional to area, so what do we make of all those thermodynamic relations that include volume, like Boyle's law or descriptions for a gas in a box? In otherwords how do we associate volume to the entropy of a Black hole?

In the previous section we defined a Black hole as a mathematical spacetime singularity that is; a position in space where quantities used to determine the gravitational field become infinite; such quantities include the curvature of spacetime and the density of matter. That is, for high or infinite densites where matter is enclosed in a very small volume of space General relativity breaks down. Quantum mechanics suggests that there may be no such thing in nature as a point in space-time, implying that space-time is always smeared out, occupying some minimum region. The minimum smeared-out volume of space-time is a profound property in any quantized theory of gravity and such an outcome lies in a widespread expectation that singularities will be resolved in a quantum theory of gravity. Therefore associating area to the entropy of a black hole means that the black hole has no volume which may not be true in a theory of quantum mechanics in curved space-time.

If density is the amount of energy contained within a given volume of space, then a Black hole must have a density and its volume will be determined by the amount os space enclosed by the surface area of its event horizon. Then from our famous equation (1) we can derive the volume entropy law of a Black hole. Let the energy density of a black hole be given as the work done on the system by exterior agents (W) per unit volume (V),

$$\rho = \frac{W}{V} = \frac{F^2}{8\pi\alpha\hbar c}$$

Since the gravitational force of a black hole is very strong and is given by, $F = \frac{c^4}{G}$. Then the work done by exterior agents on a black hole is related to its volume as,

$$W = \frac{c^7}{8\pi\alpha\hbar G^2} V = PV \qquad (6)$$

Where, P denotes the Planck pressure (or energy density) of a Black hole.

Since entropy is the quantity of heat or workdone (W) per unit temperature of a black hole (T) then from the following simple rule we derive the temperature of a Black hole as,

$$E_{pl} = NkT$$

Where, E_{pl} is the Planck energy, k is the Boltzmann constant and N is the Avagadro number given as,

$$N = \frac{W}{E_{pl}}$$

From which the temperature of a Black hole is given by

$$T = \frac{\alpha\hbar^2 G}{kc^2 V}$$

If the Black hole is a sphere with a Planck length $l_p = 1.616 \times 10^{-35} m$, then the volume of this Black hole is approximately, l_p^3. Therefore a Black hole with this volume will have the temperature $T = 1.416 \times 10^{32} K$ and this is exactly the earliest temperature in the history of the universe. Then finally the entropy of a Black hole will be given as

$$S = \frac{W}{T}$$

$$S = \frac{V^2 k c^9}{8\pi \alpha^2 \hbar^3 G^3} \approx \frac{V^2 k}{8 l_p^6} \qquad (7)$$

This reduces to the Bekenstein-Hawking area entropy law when the volume of the black hole is,

$$V = l_p^2 \sqrt{2A} \qquad (8)$$

As we said earlier the volume of a Black hole is determined by the amount of space enclosed by the surface area of its event horizon.

This section has presented a new approach to the entropy of Black holes. The major result of the research is the derivation of the volume entropy law that is different from the Bekenstein-Hawking area entropy law. As far as this book is concerned there is no other theory from which such a calculation can proceed. Hence the methods used in here are the only one from which a detailed quantum theory of gravity precedes and where the result of the volume entropy law can be achieved.

Is it Dark Matter, MOND or Quantum Black Holes?

Since the 1970s and early 1980s, a growing amount of observational data has been accumulating that shows that Newtonian and Einstein gravity cannot describe the motion of the outermost stars and gas in galaxies correctly, if only their visible mass is accounted for in the gravitational field equations.

To save Einstein's and Newton's theories, many physicists and astronomers have postulated that there must exist a large amount of "dark matter" in galaxies and also clusters of galaxies that could strengthen the pull of gravity and lead to an agreement of the theories with the data. This invisible and undetected matter removes any need to modify Newton's and Einstein's gravitational theories. Invoking dark matter is a less radical, less scary alternative for most physicists than inventing a new theory of gravity.

Fig. Galaxy data that show that Newtonian and Einstein gravity do not fit the observed speed of stars in orbits inside a galaxy such as NGC 6503

If dark matter is not detected and does not exist, then

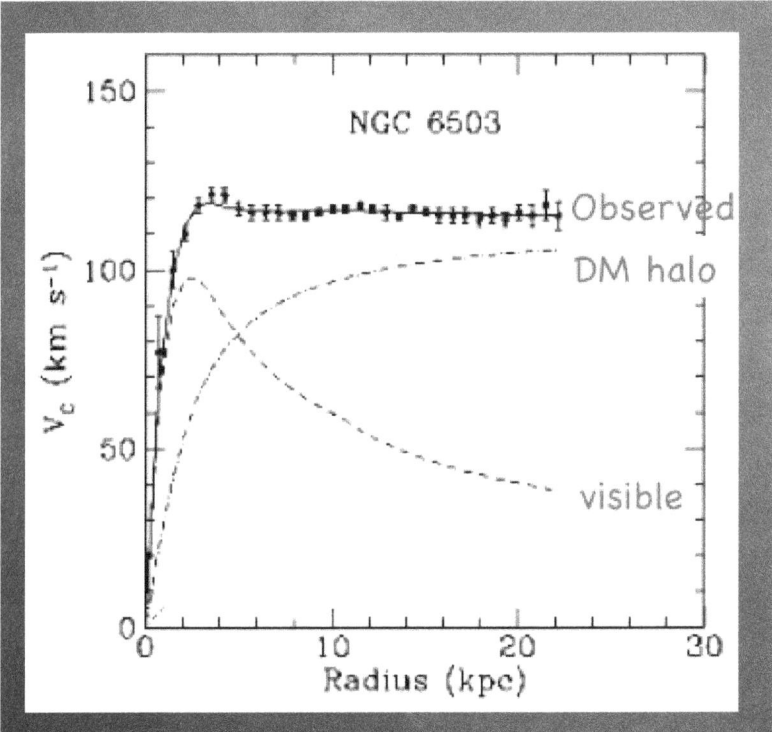

Einstein's and Newton's gravity theories must be modified. Can this be done successfully?

Yes it can be done only if we develop a theory that can determine the values of the vacuum energy density and cosmological constant which have been observed experimentally by Planck collaboration (2018) ($\rho = 5.364 \times 10^{-10} J/m^3$ and $\Lambda = 1.11 \times 10^{-52}$) with confidence.

Attempts to find a way to measure or to calculate the value of the vacuum energy density and the cosmological constant have all either failed or produced results incompatible with observations or other confirmed theoretical results. Some of those results are theoretically implausible because of certain unrealistic assumptions on which the calculation model is based. And some theoretical results are in conflict with observations, the conflict itself being caused by certain questionable hypotheses on which the theory is based. And the best experimental (Casmir effect) evidence is based on the measurement of the difference of energy density within and outside of the measuring apparatus, thus preventing in principle any numerical assessment of the actual energy density.

According to H.Sabine (2018), in the disc galaxies most of the mass is at the centre of the galaxy, this means that if you want to calculate how a star moves far away from the centre it is a good approximation to only ask what is the gravitational pull that comes from the centre bulge of the galaxy. Einstein taught us that gravity is really due to the curvature of space and time but in many cases it is still quantitatively incorrect to describe gravity as a force, this is known as the Newtonian limit and is a good approximation as long as the pull of gravity is weak and objects move much slower than the speed of light. It is a bad approximation for example close by the horizon of a black hole but it is a good approximation for the dynamics of galaxies that we are looking at here. It is then not difficult to calculate the stable orbit of a star far away from the centre of a disc galaxy. For a star to remain on its orbit, the gravitational pull must be balanced by the centrifugal force, $\frac{mv^2}{R} = \frac{GMm}{R^2}$. You can solve this equation for the velocity of the star and this will give you the velocity that is necessary for a star to remain on a stable orbit, $v = \sqrt{\frac{GM}{R}}$. As you can see the velocity drops inversely with the square root of the distance to the centre. But this is not what we observe, what we observe instead is that the velocity continue to increase with distance from the galactic centre and then they become constant.This is known as the flat rotation curve. This is not only the case for our own galaxy but it is the case for hundred of galaxies that have been observed.

The curves don't always become perfectly constant sometimes they have rigorous lines but it is abundantly clear that these observations cannot be explained by the normal matter only.

Dark matter solves this problem by postulating that there is additional mass in galaxies distributed in a spherical halo. This has the effect of speeding up the stars because the gravitational pull is now stronger due to the mass from the dark matter halo. There is always a distribution of dark matter that will reproduce whatever velocity curve we observe.

In contrast to this, Modified Newtonian Dynamics (MOND) postulates that gravity works differently. In MOND, the gravitational potential is the logarithmic of the distance $\Phi = \left(\sqrt{GMa_o}\right)\ln\left(\frac{R}{GM}\right)$, and not as normally the inverse of the distance $\Phi = \frac{-GM}{R}$. In MOND the gravitational force is then the derivation of the potential that is, the inverse of the distance $F = \frac{\sqrt{GMa_o}}{R}$, while normally it is the inverse of the square of the distance $F = \frac{GMm}{R^2}$. If you put this modified gravitational force into the force balance equation as before $\frac{\sqrt{GMa_o}}{R} = \frac{v^2}{R}$, you will see that the dependence on the distance cancels out and the velocity just becomes constant. Now of course you cannot just go and throw out the normal $\frac{1}{R^2}$ gravitational force law because we know that it works on the solar system. Therefore MOND postulates that the normal $\frac{1}{R^2}$ law crosses over into a $\frac{1}{R}$ law. This crossover happens not at a certain distance but it happens at certain acceleration. The New force law comes into play at low acceleration a_o, this acceleration where the crossover happens is a free parameter in MOND. You can determine the value of this parameter by just trying out which fits the data best. It turns out that the best fit value is closely related to the cosmological constant $a_o \approx \sqrt{\frac{\Lambda}{3}}$, why does that so? We are yet to find out but this result clearly shows that there exists an underlying principle that connects MOND to Dark matter as we are yet to find out.

Most physicists think that dark matter is a particle, similarly to the most subatomic particles that we know of like the protons, neutrons and electrons. Whatever it is, it behaves very similarly to gravity. But it doesn't emit or absorb light and it passes through normal matter undetected. We would like to know what particle it is? For example, how heavy is it? Or does anything at all happen if it interacts with normal matter? The only way we can answer the first two questions is through calculating from first principles the values of the cosmological constant as given by Planck collaborations (2018) and once our hypothesis matches with the Planck experiment then we will surely have proved what really dark matter and MOND is.

Consider the fabric of space-time to be made up of Planck mass relics or Primordial Black holes formed in the early universe after the big bang. Let these Planck particles which are the building blocks of space-time have a mass equal to the Planck mass of $M_{pl} = \sqrt{\frac{hc}{G}} = 2.18 \times 10^{-8} kg$.

Just like a gas in the box, these Planck particles are enclosed in the vaccum of space together with their antiparticle of negative mass $M_D = 2.76 \times 10^{-9} kg = 0.127 M_{pl}$.

The Planck particles are seen moving away from their antiparticle due to the Newtonian force law of $F = M_{pl} a_o$, where a_o is the low gravitational acceleration in MOND.

This movement of the Planck particles from their antiparticle is what we observe as an expanding space and hence the vacuum energy density or the cosmological constant from equation (1),

$$\rho = \frac{M_{pl}^2 a_o^2}{8\pi \alpha hc} \qquad (9)$$

Since the gravitational coupling constant is known to be $\alpha = \frac{GM_D^2}{hc}$, where M_D has a negative mass value. Putting this into account, we get the vacuum energy density value in agreement with the Planck collaboration 2018 values as,

$$\rho = \frac{a_o^2}{8\pi G}\left(\frac{M_{pl}}{M_D}\right)^2 = 5.369 \times 10^{-10} \frac{J}{m^3} \quad (10)$$

This is the main formula and central result of the cosmological constant, since it allows one to make a direct comparison with observations.

As a final fun comment let us, just out of curiosity, take the formula and apply it to the entire universe. Now we note that the critical energy density of the universe equals

$$\rho_{crit} = \frac{3H_o^2 c^2}{8\pi G} = \frac{a_o^2}{8\pi G}\left(\frac{M_{pl}}{M_D}\right)^2$$

From which we obtain a relation between a_o (MONDian-determined by fits to internal properties of galaxies), H_o is the hubble constant (a measure of the present-day expansion rate of the Universe) and α_e (coupling which determines the strength of the force) as,

$$a_o = cH_o\left(\frac{M_D}{M_{pl}}\right)\sqrt{3} \quad (11)$$

This relation holds remarkably well for the experimentally verified parameters and because it is in agreement with observations, our energy density formula (10) would be applicable to the entire universe.

The cosmological constant Λ is a dimensionful parameter with units of $(length)^{-2}$. From the point of view of classical general relativity, there is no preferred choice for what the length scale defined by Λ might be. Particle physics, however, brings a different perspective to the question. Einstein introduced a cosmological constant into his equations for General Relativity. This term acts to counteract the gravitational pull of matter, and so it has been described as an anti-gravity effect. The cosmological constant turns out to be a measure of the energy density but no one has ever calculated the cosmological constant with confidence. Previously we showed that the cosmological constant is related to the vacuum energy density by the Friedmann relationship as,

$$\Lambda = \frac{8\pi G}{c^4}\rho$$

When we substitute for (10), we get the value of the cosmological constant as,

$$\Lambda = \frac{a_o^2}{c^4}\left(\frac{M_{pl}}{M_D}\right)^2 = 1.11 \times 10^{-52} m^{-2} \qquad (12)$$

Combining (11) with (12) we obtain a relation between the Hubble constant, the low acceleration and the cosmological constant as

$$a_o = \frac{c^3}{H_o}\frac{M_D}{M_{pl}}\frac{\Lambda}{\sqrt{3}}$$

In a limit when, $\frac{M_D}{M_{pl}} = \frac{H_o}{c\sqrt{\Lambda}} = 0.6956$ (This value is so close to the experimentally defined density parameter values of $\Omega = 0.6889 \pm 0.056$ Planck2018), it turns out that the best fit value for MOND is closely related to the cosmological constant, $a_o = c^2\sqrt{\frac{\Lambda}{3}}$ and this value happens at the mass scale of $M_D = 1.5164 \times 10^{-8} kg$. This has not been confirmed experimentally but it points to the theoretical observation that dark matter is a particle of a mass close Planck mass relics (or primordial black holes) which remain whenever a black hole evaporates or those which where formed in the early universe after the big bang. The parameter a_0 is the acceleration scale introduced in the phenomenological fitting formula for galaxy rotation curves. a_o is the parameter that was introduced by Milogram in MOND. It is also an explanation for the phenomenological success of Milogram's fitting formula, in particular in reproducing the flattening of rotation curves, where the asymptotic velocity of the flattened galaxy rotation curve is, $v_f^4 = a_o GM$ this is known as the baryonic Tully-Fisher relation and has been well tested by observations of a very large number of spiral galaxies.

Therefore from general formulas and assumptions given above, we have provided a precise calculation of the cosmological parameters of ρ (vacuum energy density), Λ (Cosmological constant) and H_o (Hubble constant) in agreement with the Planck (2018) observations. We have assumed only one parameter M_D which we believe will be determined by experiment this year. The results of ρ and Λ only happen when $a_o = 1.2 \times 10^{-10} m/s^2$ and, $M_D = 2.76 \times 10^{-9} kg$. Because the parameter a_o has been determined to be a best fit for galaxy rotation curves, we therefore remain to determine by experimental means the particle with a mass M_D for galaxies and galaxy clusters. Once M_D is confirmed, the equations given will prove once and for all that the postulated Dark matter hypothesis is not responsible for what happens in galaxies and galaxy clusters.

What is real? General Relativity or Quantum Gravity

In this section we want to find out the reality behind the bending of light near the Sun's surface.

The Newtonian Approach

During Newton's time, it was believed that light was made up of particles moving at a varying speed. To prove why light bends near the Sun's surface Newton had to assume that these particles had mass. For example he considered a Sun with mass M, where a particle of light with mass m from a distant star past the Sun, had to bend near the Sun's surface due to the gravitational force of attraction acting on the particle of light. Because of this, the observer at the earth's surface never saw the actual position of the star but rather the apparent position of the star at an angle θ from its original position.

Newton assumed that, the particle of light falling freely in the gravitational field of the Sun gained kinetic energy,

$$E_k = \frac{mv^2}{2}$$

Where, v was the speed of the particle of light. The potential gravitational energy that was gained by the particle was given by,

$$V_k = \frac{GMm}{R}$$

Where R was the radius of the Sun from its centre to the point where light curved. Newton assumed that deflection angle was actually the ratio of the gravitational potential to the kinetic energy of the particle of light,

$$\theta = \frac{V_r}{E_k}$$

$$\theta = \frac{2GM}{v^2 R}$$

During Newton's time, the speed of the photon (a particle of light) was not known but, today we know this value to a much greater accuracy, thanks to Maxwell and Einstein. All the parameters, from the Sun's mass to the speed of light are known to high accuracy, therefore the Newtonian deflection angle is now known to be,

$$\theta_N = \frac{2GM}{c^2 R} = 0.875 \, arcsec$$

The problem with the Newtonian approach is this; we now know that photons of light are massless and move at a constant speed of light c and, the Newtonian deflection angle value is not in agreement with the observations. Therefore Newton's original calculation was flawed and required another explanation.

The Einstein Approach

In the Einstein approach it was found out that, the particles of light were called photons and that these particles where massles moving at a constant speed of light $c = 3 \times 10^8 m/s$.

Einstein's theory proposes that gravity is not an actual force, but is instead a geometric distortion of spacetime not predicted by ordinary Newtonian physics. The more mass you have to produce the gravity in a body the more distortion you get, this distortion changes the trajectories of objects moving through space, and even the paths of light rays, as they pass close-by the massive body. Even so, this effect is very feeble for an object as massive as our own sun, so it takes enormous care to even detect that it is occurring.

The Einstein deflection angle was twice the Newton's angle of deflection $\theta = 2\theta_N$, but there is no any account in literature where it shows the derivation of this deflection angle from Einstein field equations, which means that, Einstein came up with a formula similar to the Newtonian deflection angle formula given as,

$$\theta_E = \frac{4GM}{c^2 R} = 1.75 arcsec$$

Instead of the number, 2 in the Newton formula, we have a 4 and the varying speed of light in the Newton approach is replaced by a constant speed of light c.

The Einstein value was determined by observation through observing the solar eclipse. Although they say it agrees with experiment, we know that this is not true. It has long been suspected that the deflection of light in the vicinity of the sun exceeds the general relativistic predicted value of 1.75". An example of this, is the Erwin Finlay Freundlich 1929 solar eclipse expedition which produced a value of 2.24" larger than the general relativistic value. It is expected that once the reason for the deviation in the deflection angle has been found, it will disprove Einstein's imaginations for the curvature of space time.

It's almost hundred years since Sir Arthur Eddington experimentally proved Einstein's general relativity theory right. Since then, there has never been any competing theory that would prove Einstein wrong save for Loop quantum gravity and string theory. The fact that starlight is bent at the surface of the gravitating body by a deflection angle of 1.75" imposes a bound on the theoretical justification of gravity. Calculating an angle below or above 1.75" will be an upheaval in the founding blocks of physics. Erwin Finlay Freundlich was one of those people who stood out of the ordinary in 1929 when he published results with a larger angle of deflection than Eddington's. An account on Freundlich 1929 expedition has been clearly given in Robert J.Trumpler and Klaus Hentschel papers as stated below;

"Among the various expeditions sent out to observe the total solar eclipse of May 9, 1929, that of the Potsdam Observatory (Einstein Stiftung) seems to be the only one which obtained photographs suitable for determining the light deflection in the Sun's gravitational field. Two instruments were used, but so far only the results of the larger one, a 28-foot horizontal camera combined with a coelostat, have been published. The three observers, Freundlich, von Klüber, and von Brunn, claim that these observations (four plates containing from seventeen to eighteen star images each) lead to a value of 2.24" for the deflection of a light ray grazing the Sun's edge; a figure that deviates considerably from the results of the 1922 eclipse, and which is in contradiction to Einstein's generalized theory of relativity".

The irreducible anomaly in the observations of the deflection of light by the sun has been known to exist since the birth of Einstein General relativity theory. For example, in a 1959 classical review by A.A.Mikhailov, it concludes that observations yield instead of a general relativistic prediction of 1.75arcsec at the limb of the sun the simple mean value of 2.03 ± 0.10 over the GR prediction

The existence of a 2.24" deflection angle by Freundlich, Von Kluber and Von Brunn therefore implies a requirement for the modification of the general theory of relativity. Science has evolved in this simpler manner of modifications although there are some who cling to the old thoughts of "The earth is the center of the universe and Einstein is always right". I am not proving anyone wrong but I want you to believe that the general relativity theory that was put forward by Einstein is not the only 'there is' excellent description of the universe, there are other ways far better than GR as it was with the Newtonian Gravitational force replacement with a curvature of space time.

The introduction of a number **4** in Einstein deflection angle of light has no basis as to how it came along. The fact that his formula resembles the Newton formula actually shows that Einstein borrowed ideas from Newton analysis. He

Einstein also failed to eliminate the mass of a photon from his equations. Even today no one knows how to deduce the deflection angle without taking into account the photon mass because we know the photon is massless.

Ladies and gentlemen, let me present to you another approach that will lead us to the Einstein deflection angle without assuming that the photon has mass or kinetic energy.

Loop Quantum Gravity Approach

Let the potential energy of the Photon according to Einstein – Planck relation be,

$$E = \frac{hc}{\lambda}$$

Where λ is the wavelength

Since ligth appears curved at a small part of the Sun's surface, then the circumference according to deBrogile is quantized in units, $C=\pi R=\lambda$ (In case light orbits the Sun, then $C=2\pi R$). Then the energy of the photon will be given by

$$E_r = \frac{2\hbar c}{R}$$

According to relativistic quantum mechanics, a photon of momentum P, has a kinetic- energy given by, where M is the Sun's mass

$$E_B = \frac{P^2}{2M}$$

According to quantum mechanics in curved space time, space is divided into small chuncks of matter (atoms of space) with a length close to the Planck length l_p , therefore the momentum of a photon passing through these atoms of space will be given by,

$$P = \frac{\hbar}{l_p}$$

This momentum is proof that the photon has no mass and what we percieve as the heaviness of the photon is actually the discrete nature of space.

Due to the discrete nature of space, there is a delay in time at which the photon will reach our telescopes from the distant star. In other words the speed of light doesn't change but there is a huge difference from the calculated time and the observed time of reach of light from the distant star. Then the energy carried by a photon through the discrete space is given as

$$E_B = \frac{\hbar c^3}{2GM}$$

This then brings us to the deflection angle which is the ratio of the photon potential energy to the kinetic energy,

$$\theta = \frac{E_r}{E_B}$$

$$\theta = \frac{4GM}{c^2 R}$$

The Extra Dimension Approach

In higher dimensions or extra dimension problems we get a different picture of what general relativity really is. We assume that light behaves differently in various dimensions and the observations of light from a distant star will vary according to the flux in the extra dimensions because it is this loss of flux to the extra dimensions which makes gravity weak yet it is strong.

Therefore what determines our observations is the flux in the extra dimensions as expressed in our model below,

Let the deflection angle of light at the sun's limb be given by,

$$\theta = \frac{1}{\alpha^{n/2}}\left(\frac{R_s}{R}\right) \qquad (13)$$

Where, $R_s = \frac{2GM}{c^2}$ is the Schwarzschild radius of a gravitating body, α is the size of the extra dimension and $\alpha^{n/2}$ is the flux in the extra dimension. In what follows, we use the above equation by subsitituting in the values of $\alpha^{n/2}$ to get the values of the three deflection angles whose sample mean gives the Einstein deflection value. This analysis will help us recover new theories based on the flux in the extra dimension.

Let us start with the Newton's theory of gravitation. To recover the Newtonian deflection angle at the suns limb, we set $\alpha^{n/2} = 1$. This then gives the Newtonian value as,

$$\theta_N = \frac{R_s}{R_\odot} = 0.875 \text{arcsec}$$

The Freundlich deflection angle might have taken a different twist than with Eddington 1.75arcsec result, which we are yet to find out. Taking, $\alpha^{n/2} = 0.0233$, we deduce the deflection angle given by,

$$\theta_F = \frac{2.56 R_s}{R_\odot} = 2.24 \text{arcsec}$$

Lastly when $\alpha^{n/2} = 0.0290$ we get the following deflection angle,

$$\theta_Q = \frac{2.426 R_s}{R_\odot} = 2.12 \text{arcsec}$$

Our first result from the above calculations is that; the sample mean of the deflection angles from the three observations gives the exact deflection angle that was calculated and observed by Eddington in General relativity as,

$$\frac{\sum_{n=1}^{4} \theta_n}{3} = \frac{0.875 + 2.24 + 2.12}{3} = 1.75 arcsec$$

The fact that the mean of the three observations for the deflection of light given above reproduces the GR value of 1.75arcsec sums up what exactly general relativity really is. In simple terms GR is the sample mean of three observations taken from different location on the earth's surface where the flux in the extra dimension makes the strength of gravity slightly different in those positions where light bends.

The model given above is proof that the curvature of space assumption given by General Relatitiy was just a mathematical artifact and not a real entity. The observed deflection angles are greatly determined by the flux in the extra dimensions.

Particle Creation by Black Holes: Is it Hawking's Approach or My Approach?

In 1975 Hawking calculated quantum mechanically that a black hole will emit particles as if it were a black body with a temperature proportional to its surface gravity. Although this thermal emission is insignificant for black holes formed by stellar collapse, it is of crucial importance for the small primordial black holes formed by density fluctuations in the early universe.

The most significant consequence of a black hole is that, the temperature of a black hole increases as a black hole loses mass. The temperature increases exponentially into a burst of gamma rays leaving a black hole remnant. There is no clear account on this, not until we have fully developed a consistent quantum theory of gravity (where the mass of a black hole approaches the Planck scale of mass and radius).

The evaporation of a black hole starts with a spin down phase in which the Hawking radiation carries away the angular momentum, after which it proceeds with emission of thermally distributed quanta until the black hole reaches the Planck mass.

The radiation spectrum contains all Standard Model particles, which are emitted on our brane, as well as gravitons, which are also emitted into the extra dimensions. It is expected that most of the initial energy is emitted during this phase in Standard Model particles.

One of the major problem with black holes is that, we cannot directly measure any properties of them neither can we produce black holes in any terrestrial experiment. According to Cheung (2002), this is due to the fact that in order to produce black holes in collider experiments one needs a centre of mass energy above the Planck scale, which is obviously inaccessible at the moment. But thanks to the introduction of the numerical coefficient, we can now as this section directs, detect a vast number of black holes in our galaxy by observing and detecting the mass scale or the low energy scale quanta emitted whenever a black hole evaporates due to stellar collapse.

The numerical coefficient α depends on which particle species can be emitted at a significant rate and can be determined by taking the effect of the absorption cross section. This coefficient is of great importance in the standard model and if described in detail it could unlock the secrets hidden deep in the cosmos.

The dominant contribution to α in the standard model comes from fermions, the contribution to α for electrons and positrons is 1.575×10^{-4} (Don Page 1975).

Page calculated the emission rates for massless particles, predicted the lifetime of black holes (from the total power emitted in all modes) and also deduced the numerical coefficient for the dimensionally determined quantities (in terms of the Planck mass etc).The coefficient appears in Eqn25 and Eqn26 of the rate of change of mass and the life time of a black hole by Don Page (1975). There is no known formula relating the numerical coefficient to the mass scale or low energy scale quanta, the mass of an electron and the mass of a proton. Yet this could provide a unique probe of at least four areas of physics: the early Universe; gravitational collapse; high energy physics; and quantum gravity.

Assuming that a black hole emits particles at a mass scale M_* (low energy scale quanta), we propose the Numerical coefficient to be

$$\alpha = \frac{2M_* m_e}{m_p^2} \qquad (14)$$

Where, m_p is the mass of the Proton and m_e is the mass of an electron. This concept will help us understand the type of particles emitted by Black holes and how detecting them will help us observe most of the Black holes in space, the coeffient will be efficient in the derivation of the Chandrasekher mass limit and the Bekenstein-Hawking area entropy law. Also this coefficient will be of good use in understanding the lowest energy level of the White dwarf Hydrogen atom. In the table below, we give values of α for different mass scales M_*.

Table 1

α	Mass scale M_* (kg)	Remarks
2.837×10^{15}	4.343×10^{-9}	Planck particle-Planck scale
1	1.531×10^{-24}	Yet to be found≈ 1TeV
0.073	2.23×10^{-25}	Higgs boson
1.575×10^{-4}	2.41×10^{-28}	Pion-Neutral- cosmic rays

Note: M_{pl} (the Planck mass of $\left(\frac{\hbar c}{8\pi G}\right)^{1/2}$ =4.343 × 10^{-9}kg)

From the analysis given above, a black hole of mass M_{BH} will have a temperature and a life time given by

Temperature: $T = \frac{M_{pl}^2 c^2}{k M_{BH}} \left(\frac{2M_* m_e}{m_p^2}\right) = \frac{M_{pl}^2 c^2}{k M_{BH}} \alpha$

$$T = 8.0305 \times 10^{46} \frac{M_*}{M_{BH}}$$

Lifetime: $\tau = \frac{G M_{BH}^3 m_p^2}{M_{pl}^2 c^3 M_* m_e} = \frac{2 G M_{BH}^3}{M_{pl}^2 c^3 \alpha}$

$$\tau = 8.019 \times 10^{-43} \frac{M_{BH}^3}{M_*}$$

Note: The power of a black hole is given by, $P = \frac{M_{pl}^2 c^5}{2 G M_{BH}} \alpha$

For purposes of this study, let us limit ourselves to two Primordial Black holes, one with a mass of 4.7×10^{11}kg and another with mass 1.331×10^{17}kg. We calculate the

Temperature and life time of these black holes at known and assumed mass scales as given in table 2 and table 3.

Table 2.

Black hole (Kg)	Mass scale M_*	Temp- T(K)	τ (sec)	Remarks
4.7 × 10¹¹	4.343 × 10⁻⁹	7.42 × 10²⁶	19.17	Early universe
	1.531 × 10⁻²⁴	2.62 × 10¹¹	5.44 × 10¹⁶	Current Age of the Universe
	2.23 × 10⁻²⁵	3.81 × 10¹⁰	3.73 × 10¹⁷	Current Age of the Universe
	2.41 × 10⁻²⁸	4.12 × 10⁷	3.46 × 10²⁰	?

Note: For $M_* = M_{BH}$ we obtain the temperature of a Black hole $T = 8.0305 \times 10^{46}$ K. This is the maximum temperature of a black hole above which the black hole cease to exist.

Table 3.

Black hole (Kg)	Mass scale M_*	Temp-T(K)	τ (sec)	Remarks
1.33×10^{17}	4.343×10^{-9}	2.62×10^{21}	4.34×10^{17}	Current Age of the Universe
	1.53×10^{-24}	9.24×10^{5}	1.23×10^{33}	
	2.23×10^{-25}	1.35×10^{5}	8.46×10^{33}	
	2.41×10^{-28}	145.52	7.83×10^{36}	

We learn from the above tables that, the temperature and lifetime associated with a black hole will not only depend on the mass of a black hole but also on the mass scale of the quanta emitted as scaled from the numerical coefficient which depends on which particle species can be emitted at a significant rate. For example, the theory of black hole radiations that was developed by S.W. Hawking will only become correct and deducible to the Hawking temperature and life time formula for black holes in a limit $M_* = 1.531 \times 10^{-24}$kg and $\alpha = 1$. Such that, $T = \frac{1.229 \times 10^{23} \text{kg}}{M_{BH}}$ °K and $t = 5.238 \times 10^{-19} M_{BH}^3$. In other words M_* is assumed to be the scale of the underlying theory. The predictions of the Hawking radiations for a black hole with mass 4.7×10^{11}kg are as given in table 2 at a mass scale 1.531×10^{-24}kg. These take on similar properties for the Higgs boson. Therefore observations at such a scale could shed more light on the detection of a 4.7×10^{11}kg black hole. If we observe at a scale of a Pion $M_* = 2.41 \times 10^{-28}$kg at the current age of the universe (about 13.8×10^9yrs) we should be able to detect a black hole with a mass of 6.698×10^4kg (Primordial Black hole).

    The ideas presented above could provide a unique probe of at least four areas of physics: the early Universe;

gravitational collapse; high energy physics; and quantum gravity. The first topic is relevant because studying primordial black hole formation and evaporation can impose important constraints on primordial inhomogeneities and cosmological phase transitions. The second topic relates to recent developments in the study of "critical phenomena" and the issue of whether primordial black holes are viable dark matter candidates. The third topic arises because primordial black hole evaporations could contribute to cosmic rays, whose energy distribution would then give significant information about the high energy physics involved in the final explosive phase of black hole evaporation. The fourth topic arises because it has been suggested that quantum gravity effects could appear at the TeV scale ($M_* = 1.531 \times 10^{-24}$ kg) and this leads to the intriguing possibility that small black holes could be generated in accelerators experiments or cosmic ray events, with striking observational consequences (see B.J.Carr, 2005).

Lastly, the significance of α-the numerical coefficient can be seen in a broad sense when applied to the sun. If we take the sun to be a black hole with mass 1.99×10^{30} kg and a temperature at its center of $T = 1.5 \times 10^7$ K, we obtain a mass scale of $M_* = 3.717 \times 10^{-10}$ kg, which gives a life time of $\tau = 1.700 \times 10^{58}$ sec, the time that will be taken by the sun to dissipate if the temperature given at its center was 1.5×10^7 K.

The Chandrasekhar Mass Limit

A region in the universe has a potential energy of self-gravitation,

$$E_g = \frac{M_{pl}^2 c^2}{M_{BH}} \left(\frac{2M_* m_e}{m_p^2}\right)\left(\frac{6.144\pi^3}{\mu_e^2}\right) \quad (15)$$

A star will collapse to a White dwarf when the above energy is in equilibrium with the energy due to the electron degeneracy pressure of a Hydrogen atom given as,

$$E_e = m_e c^2 \quad (16)$$

Where $\mu_e = 2$ is the average molecular weight per electron, which depends upon the chemical composition of a star. Then for, $E_g = E_e$

$$M = \frac{12.288\pi^3}{\mu_e^2} \frac{M_{pl}^2 M_*}{m_p^2}$$

In a limit for $M_* = M_{pl}$ and $\alpha = 2.837 \times 10^{15}$, we obtain the Chandrasekhar mass limit for a white dwarf star as,

$$M = \frac{12.288\pi^3}{\mu_e^2} \frac{M_{pl}^3}{m_p^2} = 1.4 M_{sun}$$

Note that such a result is only possible in the given limit but for a limit such as $M_* = 1.531 \times 10^{-24}$ kg we obtain, $M = 4.956 \times 10^{-16} M_{sun}$ which is the mass of the Primordial black hole, providing evidence for the Hawking limit for particle emission by black holes as described previously

Planck epoch

From an expression for the life time of a black hole, it is theorized that a Black hole has a mass $M_{BH} = kM_*^{1/3}$ where k is a constant. For k=1, we have a life time of 8.019×10^{-43} sec almost the Planck time-the earliest period of time in the history of the universe).

The Bekenstein-Hawking area entropy law

From the Black hole temperature we can calculate the entropy of a black hole, the total energy of a black hole with mass M and surface area A is given as,

$$E = \frac{Ac^5 M_{pl}^2 M_* m_e}{2\pi G \hbar m_p^2 M}$$

The change in entropy when a quantity of E is added to a black hole is,

$$S = \frac{E}{T}$$

Since the temperature is known (see above) on substituting we have

$$S = \frac{Ac^3 k}{4\pi G \hbar}$$

This is the Bekenstein-Hawking area entropy formula.

The Lowest Possible Energy State of a White dwarf Hydrogen Atom

In this section we prove an existence of the minimal principal quantum number which imposes a general bound on the energy level of the Hydrogen atom and the orbital radius of an electron. The results are derived from general laws not known by the entire scientific community. The section therefore provides a relationship between the micro and macro structures of the universe at a level when the atomic mass limit is in equal proportion to the Chandrasekhar mass limit.

I won't go into details of the literature of the Chandrasekhar mass limit as these have been repeatdly written and analysed in almost a million papers about the topic. But for a brief introduction into the derivation of the Chandrasekhar mass I refer the reader to Chandrasekhar 1983 Noble prize lecture (1). Almost every aspect of a white dwarf star has been studied but there is one thing which we do not know about white dwarfs in relation to the Hydrogen atom and this is encoded in Flower's original statement;

"The black-dwarf material is best likened to a single gigantic molecule in its lowest quantum state. On the Fermi-Dirac statistics, its high density can be achieved in one and only one way, in virtue of correspondingly great energy content. But this energy can no more be expended in radiation than the energy of a normal atom or molecule. The only difference between black-dwarf matter and a normal molecule is that the molecule can exist in a free state while the black-dwarf matter can only so exist under very high external pressure"

The question is, do we have an existing relationship between the mass limit of the Hydrogen atom and the White dwarf star? If the black-dwarf material is best likened to a single gigantic molecule in its lowest quantum state, what is the lowest possible energy state at which such a relationship exists?

Briefly let us propose in formula a model to support our argument; Firstly, let the potential energy of self-gravitation of a star be given by,

$$E_g = \frac{2M_{pl}{}^3 m_e c^2}{M_S m_{pro}{}^2}\left(\frac{6.144\pi^3}{\mu_e{}^2}\right) \qquad (17)$$

Where M_{pl} is the Planck mass $\left(\frac{\hbar c}{8\pi G}\right)^{1/2}$, m_{pro} is the Proton mass, m_e electron mass, M_S mass of star and c is the constant speed of light

Lastly, the quantized energy of an Hydrogen atom is given by,

$$E_n = \frac{m_e K_e{}^2 e^4}{2n^2 \hbar^2} \qquad (18)$$

Where n is the principle quantum number which indicates the energy levels in the Hydrogen atom.

By connecting the above equations we shall be able to deduce the lowest principle quantum number in the Hydrogen atom, providing one of the first relationship between the microscope and macroscopic structures of the universe.

Equating (17) to (18) we have

$$\frac{2M_{pl}{}^3 m_e c^2}{M_S m_{pro}{}^2}\left(\frac{6.144\pi^3}{\mu_e{}^2}\right) = \frac{m_e K_e{}^2 e^4}{2n^2 \hbar^2}$$

On arranging and canceling like terms we have;

$$n = \frac{\alpha_e \mu_e m_{pro}}{2}\sqrt{\frac{M_S}{6.144\pi^3 M_{pl}{}^3}}$$

Where $\alpha_e = \frac{K_e e^2}{\hbar c} = \frac{1}{137}$ is the fine is is structure constant.

When, $M_S = 1.4 M_{sun}$ (Chandrasekhar mass limit), we have $n = 5.1586 \times 10^{-3}$. This is the allowed principal quantum number or the lowest energy state of an Hydrogen atom for a white dwarf star at the Chandrasekhar mass limit. Therefore the quantized energy of the Hydrogen atom at this principal number is

$$E_n = \frac{13.606 \text{eV}}{n^2} = 511.289 \times 10^3 \text{eV}$$

And the electron radius at this energy level is $r = 1.405 \times 10^{-15}$ m.

This result implies that, whereas the Bohr's orbital quantization doesn't permit orbits below the Bohr radius of 5.28×10^{-11} m, the theory above says that this is possible for an atom under high pressure. The electrons are therefore bound to the surface of the proton. For a white dwarf star of $M_s = 0.87 M_{sun}$, we have $n = 4.07668 \times 10^{-3}$. This gives the radius of a proton of $r = 8.775 \times 10^{-16}$ m which has been determined by spectroscopy methods.

Stellar Mass Black Holes or Primordial Holes

The smallest black hole would be one where the Schwarzschild radius equals the radius of a mass with a reduced Compton wavelength which is the smallest size to which a given mass can be localized. For a small mass M, the Compton wavelength exceeds half the Schwarzschild radius, and no black hole description exists. This smallest mass for a black hole is thus approximately the Planck mass, the micro black hole.

Contrary to the above observation, torsion (see Einstein-Cartan theory) modifies the Dirac equation in the presence of the gravitational field causing fermions to be spatially extended. This spatial extension of fermions limits the minimum mass of a black hole to be on the order of 10^{16} Kg, showing that micro black holes (of Planck mass) may not exist. Another mass limit is from the data of the Fermi Gamma-ray space telescope satellite which states that, less than one percent of dark matter could be made of primordial black holes with masses up to 10^{13} Kg.

The major aim of this section is to prove theoretically the existence of a minimum mass limit of a black hole and thereafter prove Chandrasekhar wrong (see Chandrasekhar 1983 Noble lecture concluding statement below)

"We conclude that there can be no surprises in the evolution of stars of mass less than 0.43Solarmass ($?= 2$). The end stage in the evolution of such stars can only be that of the white dwarfs. (Parenthetically, we may note here that the so-called 'mini' black-holes of mass 10^{12} Kg cannot naturally be formed in the present astronomical universe.)"

From the theory of white dwarf stars, the radius limit of a white dwarf of mass M is given by the following equation,

$$R_w = \frac{(9\pi)^{2/3}}{8} \frac{\hbar^2}{m_e G(m_{pro})^{5/3} M^{1/3}} \qquad (21)$$

Where m_{pro} and m_e is the proton and electron mass respectively

Just like the Compton wavelength, there must exist another radius for the consistitution of stars that differs from the radius given in (21) above. For example, in the same way the Planck mass is deduced (i.e by equating the Schwarzschild radius to the Compton wavelength) is the same way in which we are to prove the existence of the mass limit of a black hole.

We start from first principles. Let it be known that the derivation of the Chandrasekhar mass limit will follow the equipartition of the gravitational potential energy of a star to its electron degeneracy pressure. Where by, if the gravitational binding energy is given by,

$$E_g = \frac{2 M_{pl}^3 m_e c^2}{M m_{pro}^2} \frac{(6.144\pi^3)}{\mu^2}$$

Where M_{pl}, is the Planck mass and μ is the average molecular weight per electron

And the electron degeneracy energy pressure of the star is given by,

$$E_d = m_e c^2$$

When $E_g = E_d$ then we obtain the mass limit of the white dwarf star as,

$$M = \frac{12.288\pi^3}{\mu_e^2} \frac{M_{pl}^3}{m_p^2} = 1.4 M_{sun}$$

If then this is true, then the formula for the gravitational binding energy of a star is also true. This therefore implies that the following assumption will also be true.

When the binding gravitational energy of a star is equal to the Newtonian gravitational potential energy $\frac{GM^2}{R}$ we obtain the radius which is the smallest size to which a given mass of a star can be localized as,

$$\frac{GM^2}{R} = \frac{2M_{pl}^3 m_e c^2 (6.144\pi^3)}{Mm_{pro}^2 \mu^2}$$

$$R = \frac{Gm_{pro}^2}{2m_e c^2} \left(M/M_{pl}\right)^3 \frac{\mu^2}{6.144\pi^3} \qquad (22)$$

This can be rewritten in the form,

$$R = R_k \left(M/M_{pl}\right)^3$$

Where $R_k = 2.384 \times 10^{-53}$ m which is smaller than the Planck length of 1.62×10^{-35} m

Therefore equating Equation (21) to Equation (22) we deduce the mass limit of a black hole as,

$$M = \left(\frac{293.534\pi^{11} M_{pl}^{21}}{\mu^6 M_{pro}^{11}}\right)^{1/10} = 9.54 \times 10^{13} \text{ Kg}$$

The value is in excellent agreement with other theoretical and experimental observations. The radius of this black hole from Equation (22) is thus 2.527×10^{14} m larger than the radius of the sun of 7×10^8 m.

In conclusion therefore the end stage in the evolution of a star can only be that of the black hole with a mass 9.54×10^{13} Kg and size of 2.53×10^{14} m in contrast with the Chandrasekhar observations.

Note that the radius given by Equation (22), $R = R_k \left(M/M_{pl}\right)^3$ above is similar to the Equation for the size of the Planck star that was given by Rovelli and Vidotto, $r = l_p \left(\frac{M}{M_{pl}}\right)^n$ where l_p is the Planck length and n is the positive number. This is a clear indication that there is a length that is smaller than the Planck length.

Additional Readings

Hidden in Plain sight1: A Simple Link between Quantum Mechanics and Relativity

The Einstein field equation is written in the form, $G_{\mu\nu} + \Lambda g_{\mu\nu} = \frac{8\pi G}{c^4} T_{\mu\nu}$ where, the expression on the left represents the curvature of space time while the expression on the right represents the matter-energy content of the universe. Then assuming a quantum state in which a gravitating particle of radius R is acted upon by all classical forces, the expression on the left, the metric of space time curvature can be written in a special form as,

$$G_{\mu\nu} + \Lambda g_{\mu\nu} = \frac{\hbar c}{F_u R^4} \qquad (23)$$

Where, F_u is the force arising from a quantized field in zero point vacuum energy, $\hbar$ is the reduced planck constant and c is the constant speed of light.

Whereas the expression on the right (the stress-energy tensor) will be written in a form,

$$T_{\mu\nu} = \frac{F_G F_E}{F_u R^2} \qquad (24)$$

Where, F_G is the Newtonian classical gravitational force between two particles of mass m, F_E is the electrostatic force between two particles of charge q and G is the gravitational constant.

Then in terms of the pressure and energy density the stress-energy tensor is,

$$T_{\mu\nu} = P_g \varphi = \rho_E \varphi$$

Where $\varphi = \frac{F_E}{F_u}$ is the coupling of forces, P_g is the pressure ($P_g = \frac{GM^2}{R^4}$) and ρ_E is the energy density or the potential gravitational energy per unit volume R^3.

Then in its simple form, the Einstein Field equation may be expressed as,

$$\frac{\hbar c}{F_E R^4} = \frac{8\pi G}{c^4} P_g = \frac{8\pi G}{c^4} \rho_E \qquad (25)$$

From the above equation, the gravitational potential field is analogous to the quantum gravitational potential by

$$\nabla^2 \phi = 4\pi G \rho_E \text{ (Classical)}$$

$$\text{And, } \nabla^2 \phi = \frac{\hbar c^5}{2 F_E R^4} \text{ (quantum)}$$

We have coupled a quantum system to a classical one by simply denoting the metric of space time in Einstein's field equation as $\frac{\hbar c}{F_u R^4}$, this out come gives us a unique technique through which we can express the gravitational effects in terms of quantum mechanics.

Einstein Field Equation for a Relationship between the DeBrogile Wavelength and the Energy Density of an Electromagnetic Wave

In a cyclotron the acceleration of a particle describing circular motion at a distance R in a magnetic field B will be given as

$$a_x = \frac{2\pi B v R}{q\mu_0},$$

Where μ_0 is the permeability of free space
q is the charge on a particle and
v is a velocity at right angles to the direction of the field B

But when quantum and gravitational effects are taken into account, we are led to a different formula for the acceleration given by

$$a_y = \frac{\hbar c^5}{8\pi G m R^2 E q},$$

This is deduced from equation18 where, the electrostatic force on a charge q in vicinity of the electric field E is $F_E = Eq$, E=Bc and the inertial force is $F_G = m a_y$.

Then at a point where the two accelerations are equal that is, $a_x = a_y$, we are led to,

$$\frac{\lambda}{2\pi R^3} = \left(\frac{8\pi G}{c^4}\right)\frac{EB}{\mu_0 c} = \left(\frac{8\pi G}{c^4}\right)\rho$$

Where $\rho = \frac{EB}{\mu_0 c}$ is the energy density of an electromagnetic wave in vacuum and $\lambda = \frac{\hbar}{mv}$ is the deBrogile wave length

The formula obtained above is the solution to the Einstein field equation in which the wave properties of matter in terms of the DE Brogile wavelength are related to the wave properties of an electromagnetic wave in terms of the energy density of an electromagnetic wave. The expression on the left represents the quantum nature of wave mechanics while that on the right represents the classical nature of electromagnetic waves interrelated by the gravitational constant.

It is therefore true from our derivations that, when the classical acceleration of particles in the cyclotron is equal in magnitude to the modern acceleration (not yet observed), we deduce properties of a wave on both a quantum and classical realm simultaneously. This means that both the wave and particle properties of matter cannot be separated in any experiment and or observation, hence a wave –particle duality of matter.

Derivation of the Schwarzschild-Hawking Power Law

Suppose a force F_E does work on a Black hole of mass M to move it through a small displacement Δd in time Δt, where $\Delta d / \Delta t$ is the average speed v, then the power is,

$$P = F_E v$$

But from equation 18, $F_E = \frac{\hbar c^5}{8\pi G^2 M^2}$, is the force required to displace or accelerate a black hole, the force increases as the mass of the black hole decreases.

If we let $v = c$ then the power of a Black hole will be given by,

$$P = \frac{\hbar c^6}{8\pi G^2 M^2}$$

This sets a limit to which velocity a black hole can be accelerated. Note: the above formula has not yet been derived in the frame work of semi classical gravity. If this is semi classical gravity, then we are towards achieving a quantum theory of gravity. I therefore leave the derivation above to the entire scientific community to investigate.

However the expression above differs from that deduced from the Stefan-Boltzmann radiation power law of

$$P = \frac{\hbar c^6}{15360\pi G^2 M^2}.$$

Meaning that, it requires a velocity of $1.5625 \times 10^5 m/s$ to obtain this power from our derivations.

Derivation of the Bekenstein –Hawking Area Entropy Law

The energy or work done by a black hole will to a great degree depend on the surface area of the event horizon A and on the Compton wavelength λ of a black hole provided the force exerted on this black hole remains a constant as,

$$W = F_E \frac{A}{\lambda}$$

The Compton wavelength is $\lambda = \frac{2\pi\hbar}{mc}$, and F_E is known, thus the energy is,

$$W = \frac{Ac^6}{16\pi^2 G^2 m}$$

This implies that, the energy of a black hole is proportional to the surface area of the event horizon but inversely proportional to its mass.

If we apply the above statement to entropy which is energy per unit temperature, S=W/T we can deduce the entropy of a black hole. Let us deduce the expression for temperature: when the electric force applied on a body of mass m through a schwarzichild's radius $R_s = \frac{2Gm}{c^2}$, results into an energy equal to the translational kinetic energy as, $F_E R_s = kT$, where k is the Boltzmann's constant. Then the expression for temperature will be given as, $T = \frac{\hbar c^3}{4\pi Gmk}$, this is the temperature of a black hole. Then substituting for the energy and temperature in the entropy formula we obtain,

$$S = \frac{Ac^3 k}{4\pi G\hbar}$$

This is the entropy of a black hole in its simplest form.

In conclusion, the Book has presented a new approach to Quantum Gravity that is different from string theory and loop quantum gravity by Carlo Rovelli and Edward Witten. The major result of the research is the derivation of the Bekenstein-Hawking area entropy law from first principles using new methods with a well defined calculation where no infinities appear. As far as this book is concerned there is no other theory from which such a calculation can proceed. Hence the methods used in here are the only one from which a detailed quantum theory of gravity "Holy Grail of modern physics" precedes and where the result of the Bekenstein-Hawking area entropy law can be achieved.

Hidden in Plain sight2: From White Dwarfs to Black Holes

A precise and consistent quantum theory of gravity has not yet been proved, not even by the self proclaimed geniuses of this time. We are aware and satisfied that classical General Relativity is the most precise description of gravity due to its predictable nature. The left hand side of Einstein field equation represents the metric of space time curvature while the right hand side represents the matter - energy content of the classical matter fields of pressure and energy density. It is known that quantum mechanics plays an important role in the behaviour of the matter fields but has no place in the Einsteins field equations. According to S.W.Hawking (1975), one therefore has a problem of defining a consistent scheme in which the space time metric is treated classically but is coupled to the matter fields which are treated quantum mechanically. In this book we propose that, in order to estimate stellar parameters to a high degree of accuracy for both microscopic and macroscopic descriptions of white dwarfs and black holes one has to treat the right hand side of Einstein field equation quantum mechanically as,

$$\left(\frac{8\pi G}{c^3}\right)^{3/2} \frac{m_H}{\hbar^{1/2}} P_{eg}$$

$P_{eg} = \frac{f_e f_g}{\hbar c}$, where P_{eg} is the total pressure, f_g is the gravitational force, f_e is the electric force, G is the gravitational constant, c is the constant speed of light, $\hbar$ is the reduced planck constant and m_H is the mass of an Hydrogen atom.

Proof of the Chandrasker Mass Limit and the Lowest Principal Quantum Number from a New Approach to Quantum Gravity

Although in the Bohr theory of an hydogen atom orbit quantization doesnot permit a lower orbit than the bohr radius of $a_o = 0.53\text{Å}$, this section sets out to show that this is not the case with white dwarfs due to the state of a hydrogen atom under high pressure.

We know from the Chandrasker derivations that, the equation governing the hydrostatic equilbrium of a star is given by

$$-r^2 P(r) = GM(r)\rho(r) \text{ or } r\frac{dP}{dr} = -\frac{GM(r)}{r^2}\rho$$

Where P denotes the total pressure, ρ is density, and M(r) is the mass interior to a sphere of radius r.

We could however write the same equation in a different form given by

$$P_{eg} r^2 = \frac{\hbar^{1/2} c^{9/2}}{(8\pi G)^{3/2} m_H} \quad (26)$$

where $P_{eg} = \frac{f_e f_g}{\hbar c}$

The total Gravitational Binding Energy of a Star

The electric potential energy $E_e = f_e r$ as we know it can be can be deduced from (26) and is given by,

$$E_e = \left(\frac{\hbar}{8\pi G}\right)^{3/2} \frac{c^{11/2}}{E_g m_H}$$

where E_g is the gravitational potential binding energy given by $f_g r$

Using the principle of energy equipartition, we assume that the electric binding energy is of order the discrete energy of an hydrogen atom from Bohrs theory as,

$$E_n = E_e \Rightarrow \left(\frac{\hbar}{8\pi G}\right)^{3/2} \frac{c^{11/2}}{E_g m_H} = \frac{m_H k_e^2 e^4}{2n^2 \hbar^2}$$

where, k_e is the Coulomb constant, e is the charge on an electron and n is the principal quantum number.

From the above assumptions the gravitational binding energy is given as,

$$E_g = 2\left(\frac{\hbar c}{8\pi G}\right)^{3/2} \left(\frac{nc}{\alpha_e m_H}\right)^2 \qquad (27)$$

where α_e is the fine structure constant $\frac{ke^2}{\hbar c} = 1/137$

In Table 1 we list the values of E_g for several values of n-the principal quantum number. From this table it follows in particular, that the higher the principal quantum number, the higher the gravitational binding energy of a star.

The total gravitational binding energy of a star

n(Principal quantum number)	E_g (Joules)	Remarks
0.003212	3.229 × 10^{47}	
0.0345	3.468 × 10^{48}	White Dwarf
1	1.005 × 10^{50}	

What do we conclude from the foregoing calculation? We conclude that equation (27) is at the base of the equilbrium of actual stars in relation to the energy state and binding energy of the Hydrogen atom. It differs from the Chandrasker calculation by the introduction of a natural fine structure constant, providing the energy of proper magnitude for the measurement of stellar energies and therefore proving to be a better theory for stellar structure. This could be elaborated in detail by flowers original words,

"The Black-dwarf material is best likened to a single gigantic molecule in its lowest quantum state. On the Fermi-Dirac statistics, its high density can be achieved in one and only one way, in virtue of a correspondingly great energy content. But this energy can no more be expended in radiation than the energy of a normal atom or molecule. The only difference between Black-dwarf matter and a normal molecule is that the molecule can exist in afree state while the black dwarf matter can only so exist under high external pressure.

The Theory of White-Dwarf Stars and Black Holes; The Limiting Mass at the Lowest Principal Quantum Number

The gravitational energy is known to be of order $E_g = \dfrac{GM^2}{r}$, M being the mass of a star. Then equating this to equation (25) we obtain the radius of a star as,

$$r = \frac{1}{2}\left(\frac{8\pi G}{\hbar c}\right)^{3/2} \left(\frac{\alpha_e m_H}{nc}\right)^2 GM^2 \quad (28)$$

while the above equation states that the radius is proportional to the square of it's mass, the Chandrasker analysis is in disagreement, stating that r is inversely proportional to the cube root of the mass.

But at a point where r equation (28) approaches the schwarzichilds radius r_s

$$r \Rightarrow r_s \, , \frac{1}{2}\left(\frac{8\pi G}{\hbar c}\right)^{3/2} \left(\frac{\alpha_e m_H}{nc}\right)^2 GM^2 = \frac{2GM}{c^2}$$

We obtain an upper limit to the mass of,

$$M = 4\left(\frac{n}{\alpha_e}\right)^2 \left(\frac{\hbar c}{8\pi G}\right)^{3/2} \frac{1}{M_H{}^2} \quad (29)$$

Now consider equating the original solution of Chandrasker mass limit to our newly developed formula (29), we have

$$M_C = M,$$

$$\frac{\omega^0{}_3 \sqrt{3\pi}}{2}\left(\frac{\hbar c}{8\pi G}\right)^{\frac{3}{2}} \frac{1}{\mu_e{}^2 M_H{}^2} = 4\left(\frac{n}{\alpha_e}\right)^2 \left(\frac{\hbar c}{8\pi G}\right)^{3/2} \frac{1}{M_H{}^2}$$

$$n = \frac{\alpha_e}{\mu_e}\left(\frac{\omega^0{}_3}{8}\sqrt{3\pi}\right)^{1/2}$$

$\omega^0{}_3 = 2.018236$, is a constant connected with the solution to the lane-Emden equation, and $\mu_e = 2$, average molecular weight per electron, then

$$n = 3.212 \times 10^{-3}$$

In the table below we list the values of M and r for several values of n-the principal quantum number, including the one calculated above.

The Mass limit and radius limit of a star

n(Principal quantum number)	M(Kilograms)	r (meters)	Remarks
3.212×10^{-3}	2.304×10^{28}	34.153	($0.012 M_{sun}$
0.0345	2.66×10^{30}	3944.601	Chandrasekar mass limit ($1.4 M_{sun}$
1	2.234×10^{33}	3.31×10^6	Maximum mass of a white dwarf

What do we conclude from the foregoing calculation? We conclude that the formation of a white dwarf star or any other stellar structure will never exceed the Schwarzichild's radius of 34.153m, this will only happen at the most lowest quantum principal number of 3.212×10^{-3}. For example, at the principal quantum number the size of the fine structure constant $\frac{1}{137}$, the mass obtained will be of $0.063 M_{sun}$ and r=176.443m. Therefore under high external pressure the minimum mass of a last star that is formed is of order $2.304 \times 10^{28} kg$ and this only occurs at r=34.153m under the lowest energy state below the known Bohrs radius of $a_o = 0.53$Å.

What is Wrong With Hawking Temperature

In his paper "Particle creation by Black holes" Hawking pointed out that "In the classical theory black holes can only absorb and not emit particles. However it is shown that quantum mechanical effects cause black holes to create and emit particles as if they were hot bodies with temperature $\frac{\hbar c^3}{8\pi GMk} \approx 10^{-6} \left(\frac{M_{sun}}{M}\right)^o K$". However this is not the case when the assumptions given in the first sections of this book are taken into account. For example, we know that, the electric potential energy is given by,

$$E_e = \left(\frac{\hbar}{8\pi G}\right)^{3/2} \frac{c^{11/2}}{E_g m_H}$$

But treating the particles in the process General relativisticaly (at the Schwarzichild radius), the gravitational potential energy will be of order $E_g = \frac{mc^2}{2}$, giving the electric energy as,

$$E_e = 2\left(\frac{\hbar}{8\pi G}\right)^{3/2} \frac{c^{7/2}}{mm_H}$$

Now the thermal energy is given by $E_{thermal} = kT$, where k is the Boltzmann constant.
By the principal of Equipartition

$$E_{thermal} \sim E_e \Rightarrow T = 2\left(\frac{\hbar}{8\pi G}\right)^{\frac{3}{2}} \frac{c^{\frac{7}{2}}}{kmm_H}, \qquad (30)$$

$$T = 3.3891 \times 10^{11} \frac{M_{sun}}{M}$$

Note: in a limit where m_H is the planck mass $m_H = \sqrt{\frac{\hbar c}{8\pi G}}$, equation (30) above for the temperature of a black hole reduces to the hawking temperature formula $T = \frac{\hbar c^3}{8\pi G M k}$

For conditions at the centre of the Sun, $T = 3.3891 \times 10^{11} K$ which is in disagreement with the Hawking temperature of $T_H = 6.476 \times 10^{-8} K$. This is left for the reader to analyse.

Entropy of a Black Hole

For derivations which i will not show here, I am led to the total energy of a Black Hole given by,

$$E_B = \frac{2A(\hbar c^{13})^{1/2}}{(8\pi G)^{5/2} m_H m}$$

where, A is the surface area of the event horizon
But since the entropy is energy per unit temperature,

$$S = \frac{E_B}{T}$$

Remember that temperature is given by equation(28),

Then the entropy will be given by,

$$S = \frac{A c^3 k}{4\pi G \hbar}$$

This is in agreement with the Bekenstein-Hawking area entopy law

On the Development of a Quantum Gravity-Hydrostatic Equation and its Implication to Physics-Minimum Black hole mass

It is known that the equation governing the hydrostatic equilibrium of a star is given by,

$$\frac{dP}{dr} = -\frac{GM(r)}{r^2}\rho \qquad (31)$$

Where P denotes the total pressure, ρ is density, and M(r) is the mass interior to a sphere of radius r.
what if we rewrite the above formula in a form given by,

$$\frac{F_g F_e}{\hbar c} r^2 = \frac{c^4}{8\pi G} = constant \qquad (32)$$

Where F_g is the gravitational force, F_e is the electric force, c is the speed of light, $\hbar$ is the reduced Planck constant and G is the gravitational constant. Let the pressure be, $P = \frac{F_g F_e}{\hbar c}$, this means that pressure is dependent on the product of the gravitational and electric forces in a quantum-relativistic realm. Therefore in simple terms, we can write (32) in its simplest form as, $\frac{dP}{dr} = -\frac{c^4}{8\pi G r^2}(r)$ and to include the density, we have

$$\frac{dP}{dr} = -\frac{rc^2}{8\pi G r_s}(r)\rho$$

where r_s is schwarzichild's radius. thus at $r_s = r$, the star will form a black hole.

To differ from (31) we have formulated one of the first quantum gravity -hydrostatic equation. From (32) we can write the electric potential energy as,

$$F_e r = \frac{\hbar c^5}{8\pi G E_g}$$

where, $E_g = F_g r$ is the gravitational potential energy at a point where the potential gravitational energy is in equilibrium with the potential electric energy the total energy is that of the Planck energy by,

$$E = F_e r = E_g = \sqrt{\frac{\hbar c^5}{8\pi G}} = 3.91 \times 10^8 J$$

since the Bohr energy of an hydrogen atom is given by,

$$E_n = \frac{m k_e^2 e^4}{2n^2 \hbar^2}$$

then, using the principle of equipartition of energy

$$F_e r = E_n$$

we deduce, the gravitational potential energy as

$$E_g = \frac{2n^2 \hbar^3 c^5}{8\pi G m_e k_e^2 e^4}$$

this can be written in a simplest form as,

$$E_g = \frac{2n^2}{m_e} \left(\frac{J_p}{\alpha_e}\right)^2 \qquad (33)$$

where, $J_p = \sqrt{\frac{\hbar c^3}{8\pi G}}$ is the planck momentum $1.3035 N.s$
$\alpha_e = \frac{k e^2}{\hbar c}$ is the fine structure constant $\frac{1}{137}$
m_e is the mass of an electron $9.11 \times 10^{-31} kg$

Then the total gravitational energy is calculated to be,

$$E_g = 7.00 \times 10^{34} J(n^2)$$

For a thermal energy kT, we estimate a temperature of

$$T = \frac{7.00 \times 10^{34}}{k} = 5.07 \times 10^{57} K$$

We know that, the gravitational potential energy is given by, $\frac{GM^2}{r}$, and for

$$E_g = \frac{GM^2}{r} = \frac{2n^2}{m_e}\left(\frac{J_p}{\alpha_e}\right)^2$$

The radius mass relation can be written as,

$$r = \frac{GM^2 m_e}{2n^2}\left(\frac{\alpha_e}{J_p}\right)^2$$

$$r = 9.527 \times 10^{-46} \frac{M^2}{n^2}$$

For the solar mass $M = 1.9 \times 10^{30} kg$, $r \sim 3.44 \times 10^{15} m$ and if r is equal to the schwarzichilds radius $\frac{GM}{c^2}$, then

$$\frac{GM}{c^2} = \frac{GM^2 m_e}{2n^2}\left(\frac{\alpha_e}{J_p}\right)^2$$

The solar mass limit is given by

$$M = \frac{2n^2}{m_e c^2}\left(\frac{J_p}{\alpha_e}\right)^2 \sim 7.78 \times 10^{17} kg$$

But for $r = \frac{2\pi \hbar}{m_e c}$, compton wavelength then

61

$$\frac{2\pi\hbar}{m_e c} = \frac{GM^2 m_e}{2n^2}\left(\frac{\alpha_e}{J_p}\right)^2$$

From which mass reduces to,

$$M = \frac{2n\hbar^{1/2}\pi^{1/2}}{G^{1/2}m_e c}\frac{J_p}{\alpha_e} \sim 2.913 \times 10^{12}\,\text{kg}$$

This is the minimum mass of a Black hole

Appendix 1

Derivation of the Energy density stored in the Electric field and Gravitational Field

We know that the electric field store energy, and that in a vacuum the energy density is given by, $\rho = \frac{\varepsilon_0}{2} E^2$ where E is the electric Field and ε_0 the permittivity of free space. If our new formula for the enegy density given in the first section of this book (Eqn1) is true, it must be able to reproduce the expression for the energy density of the electric field and also solve other problems.

To derive the energy density in the electric field, we let the force on the particle say an electron with charge e due to the electric field E created by another charged electron be, F=eE. Then the energy density will be related to the electric field by,

$$\rho = \frac{e^2 E^2}{8\pi\alpha\hbar c}$$

But because the coupling constant of the electromagnetic force is the fine structure constant $\alpha = \frac{e^2}{4\pi\varepsilon_0 \hbar c}$, then on substitution and cancelling like terms, we recover the energy density in the electric field as,

$$\rho = \frac{\varepsilon_0}{2} E^2$$

Similary, for the energy density in the gravitational field, let the force experienced by a particle of mass m due to the gravitational field g be F=mg. The energy density is here given by,

$$\rho = \frac{m^2 g^2}{8\pi\alpha\hbar c}$$

But because the coupling constant of the gravitational force is the fine structure constant- $\alpha = \frac{Gm^2}{\hbar c}$, then on substitution and cancelling like terms, we recover the energy density in the gravitational field as,

$$\rho = \frac{g^2}{8\pi G}$$

We have shown that, just as the electromagnetic field stores energy, the same is also true for the gravitational field.

Epilogue

I hope that this book has succeeded in describing to you, the reader, how difficult it is to try to wrest precious, fundamental secrets from nature. That quest can be compared to climbing a mountain, and when reaching the peak, seeing another higher mountain that tempts us to ascend to even greater heights. And when we do reach the higher peak, we discover as we look across the valley yet another peak that calls. In the end, it is the wonderful experience of scaling the mountain—of attempting to understand the secrets of nature—that motivates us as scientists. There is of course the additional thrill, upon reaching the top of a mountain, to ram in the flagpole announcing one's victory. But that is only a momentary emotion soon superseded by the new challenges presented by the higher peak on the horizon.

For readers who have a background in physics, let us think about Einstein's gravitational theory in an abstract, whole sense. Then let us think about QG. Do we get the same aesthetic pleasure from considering QG as we do from Einstein's gravity theory? To reach a true appreciation of the elegance of QG as a gravity theory, it is necessary to explore all the technical details of QG and see how it works as a whole theoretical framework. One has to experience its successes in explaining data and naturally allowing for a cosmology with no singularity at the beginning of the universe, and no dark matter, and a unified description of the accelerating universe. Only after the laborious work of achieving a technical understanding of QG's theoretical structure can one truly appreciate QG's elegance. I hope that future generations of physicists will be motivated to study the theory in the same depth as Carlo Rovelli, Joel Brownstein, and I have done, and appreciate its intrinsic beauty.

There is still important research to perform before we have a complete picture of where we stand with quantum gravity. Perhaps with more attention being paid by other physicists who can investigate QG and apply it to other observational data, we will arrive at a more convincing state-of-the-art of gravity. The ultimate tests for QG, or any alternative gravity theory, can be stated simply: With a minimum number of assumptions that are physically consistent, how much observational data can be explained? More important, can the theory make testable predictions that cannot be accounted for by competing theories? In the latter part of this book, I have suggested several ways that future observations and experiments can verify or falsify QG.

In probing the mysteries of nature, physicists need to have faith that we can through mathematical equations reach a true understanding of nature such that the predictions of our equations can be verified by experiment or observation. We need to continually aspire to that goal despite the modern trend in theoretical physics of indulging in speculations that can never be proved or falsified by reality.

Glossary

Absolute space and time—the Newtonian concepts of space and time, in which space is independent of the material bodies within it, and time flows at the same rate throughout the universe without regard to the locations of different observers and their experience of "now."

Acceleration—the rate at which the speed or velocity of a body changes.

Accelerating universe—the discovery in 1998, through data from very distant supernovae, that the expansion of the universe in the wake of the big bang is not slowing down, but is actually speeding up at this point in its history; groups of astronomers in California and Australia independently discovered that the light from the supernovae appears dimmer than would be expected if the universe were slowing down.

Action—the mathematical expression used to describe a physical system by requiring only the knowledge of the initial and final states of the system; the values of the physical variables at all intermediate states are determined by minimizing the action.

Anthropic principle—the idea that our existence in the universe imposes constraints on its properties; an extreme version claims that we owe our existence to this principle.

Asymptotic freedom (or safety)—a property of quantum field theory in which the strength of the coupling between elementary particles vanishes with increasing energy and/or decreasing distance, such that the elementary particles approach free particles with no external forces acting on them; moreover for decreasing energy and/or increasing distance between the particles, the strength of the particle force increases indefinitely.

Baryon—a subatomic particle composed of three quarks, such as the proton and neutron.

Big bang theory—the theory that the universe began with a violent explosion of spacetime, and that matter and energy originated from an infinitely small and dense point.

Big crunch—similar to the big bang, this idea postulates an end to the universe in a singularity.

Binary stars—a common astrophysical system in which two stars rotate around each other; also called a "double star."

Blackbody—a physical system that absorbs all radiation that hits it, and emits characteristic radiation energy depending upon temperature; the concept of blackbodies is useful, among other things, in learning the temperature of stars.

Black hole—created when a dying star collapses to a singular point, concealed by an "event horizon;" the black hole is so dense and has such strong gravity that nothing, including light, can escape it; black holes are predicted by general relativity, and though they cannot be "seen," several have been inferred from astronomical observations of binary stars and massive collapsed stars at the centers of galaxies.

Boson—a particle with integer spin, such as photons, mesons, and gravitons, which carries the forces between fermions.

Brane—shortened from "membrane," a higher-dimensional extension of a onedimensional string.

Cassini spacecraft—NASA mission to Saturn, launched in 1997, that in addition to making detailed studies of Saturn and its moons, determined a bound on the variations of Newton's gravitational constant with time.

Causality—the concept that every event has in its past events that caused it, but no event can play a role in causing events in its past.

Classical theory—a physical theory, such as Newton's gravity theory or Einstein's general relativity, that is concerned with the macroscopic universe, as opposed to theories concerning events at the submicroscopic level such as quantum mechanics and the standard model of particle physics.

Copernican revolution—the paradigm shift begun by Nicolaus Copernicus in the early sixteenth century, when he identified the sun, rather than the Earth, as the center of the known universe.

Cosmic microwave background (CMB)—the first significant evidence for the big bang theory; initially found in 1964 and studied further by NASA teams in 1989 and the early 2000s, the CMB is a smooth signature of microwaves everywhere in the sky, representing the "afterglow"of the big bang: Infrared light produced about 400,000 years after the big bang had redshifted through the stretching of spacetime during fourteen billion years of expansion to the microwave part of the electromagnetic spectrum, revealing a great deal of information about the early universe.

Cosmological constant—a mathematical term that Einstein inserted into his gravity field equations in 1917 to keep the universe static and eternal; although he later regretted this and called it his "biggest blunder," cosmologists today still use the cosmological constant, and some equate it with the mysterious dark energy.

Coupling constant—a term that indicates the strength of an interaction between particles or fields; electric charge and Newton's gravitational constant are coupling constants.

Crystalline spheres—concentric transparent spheres in ancient Greek cosmology that held the moon, sun, planets, and stars in place and made them revolve around the Earth; they were part of the western conception of the universe until the Renaissance.

Curvature—the deviation from a Euclidean spacetime due to the warping of the geometry by massive bodies.

Dark energy—a mysterious form of energy that has been associated with negative pressure vacuum energy and Einstein's cosmological constant; it is hypothesized to explain the data on the accelerating expansion of the universe; according to the standard model, the dark energy, which is spread uniformly throughout the universe, makes up about 70 percent of the total mass and energy content of the universe.

Dark matter—invisible, not-yet-detected, unknown particles of matter, representing about 30 percent of the total mass of matter according to the standard model; its presence is

necessary if Newton's and Einstein's gravity theories are to fit data from galaxies, clusters of galaxies, and cosmology; together, dark
matter and dark energy mean that 96 percent of the matter and energy in the universe is invisible.

Deferent—in the ancient Ptolemaic concept of the universe, a large circle representing the orbit of a planet around the Earth.

Doppler principle or **Doppler effect**—the discovery by the nineteenth-century Austrian scientist Christian Doppler that when sound or light waves are moving toward an observer, the apparent frequency of the waves will be shortened, while if they are moving away from an observer, they will be lengthened; in astronomy this means that the light emitted by galaxies moving away from us is redshifted, and that from nearby galaxies moving toward us is blueshifted.

Dwarf galaxy—a small galaxy (containing several billion stars) orbiting a larger galaxy; the Milky Way has over a dozen dwarf galaxies as companions, including the Large Magellanic Cloud and Small Magellanic Cloud.

Dynamics—the physics of matter in motion.

Electromagnetism—the unified force of electricity and magnetism, discovered to be the same phenomenon by Michael Faraday and James Clerk Maxwell in the nineteenth century.

Electromagnetic radiation—a term for wave motion of electromagnetic fields which propagate with the speed of light—300,000 kilometers per second—and differ only in wavelength; this includes visible light, ultraviolet light, infrared radiation,
X-rays, gamma rays, and radio waves.

Electron—an elementary particle carrying negative charge that orbits the nucleus of an atom.

Eötvös experiments—torsion balance experiments performed by Hungarian Count Roland von Eötvös in the late nineteenth and early twentieth centuries that showed that inertial and gravitational mass were the same to one part in 1011; this was a more accurate determination of the equivalence principle than results achieved by Isaac Newton and, later, Friedrich Wilhelm Bessel.

Epicycle—in the Ptolemaic universe, a pattern of small circles traced out by a planet at the edge of its "deferent" as it orbited the Earth; this was how the Greeks accounted for the apparent retrograde motions of the planets.

Equivalence principle—the phenomenon first noted by Galileo that bodies falling in a gravitational field fall at the same rate, independent of their weight and composition; Einstein extended the principle to show that gravitation is identical (equivalent) to acceleration.

Escape velocity—the speed at which a body must travel in order to escape a strong gravitational field; rockets fired into orbits around the Earth have calculated escape velocities, as do galaxies at the periphery of galaxy clusters.

Ether (or aether)—a substance whose origins were in the Greek concept of "quintessence," the ether was the medium through which energy and matter moved, something more than a vacuum and less than air; in the late nineteenth century the Michelson-Morley experiment disproved the existence of the ether.

Euclidean geometry—plane geometry developed by the third-century bc Greek mathematician Euclid; in this geometry, parallel lines never meet.

Fermion—a particle with half-integer spin, like protons and electrons, that make up matter.

Field—a physical term describing the forces between massive bodies in gravity and electric charges in electromagnetism; Michael Faraday discovered the concept of field when studying magnetic conductors.

Field equations—differential equations describing the physical properties of interacting massive particles in gravity and electric charges in electromagnetism; Maxwell's equations for electromagnetism and Einstein's equations of gravity are prominent examples in physics.

Fifth force or **"skew" force**—a new force in MOG that has the effect of modifying gravity over limited length scales; it is carried by a particle with mass called the phion.

Fine-tuning—the unnatural cancellation of two or more large numbers involving an absurd number of decimal places, when one is attempting to explain a physical phenomenon; this signals that a true understanding of the physical phenomenon has not been achieved.

Fixed stars—an ancient Greek concept in which all the stars were static in the sky, and moved around the Earth on a distant crystalline sphere.

Frame of reference—the three spatial coordinates and one time coordinate that an observer uses to denote the position of a particle in space and time.

Galaxy—organized group of hundreds of billions of stars, such as our Milky Way.

Galaxy cluster—many galaxies held together by mutual gravity but not in as organized a fashion as stars within a single galaxy.

Galaxy rotation curve—a plot of the Doppler shift data recording the observed velocities of stars in galaxies; those stars at the periphery of giant spiral galaxies are observed to be going faster than they "should be" according to Newton's and Einstein's gravity theories.

General relativity—Einstein's revolutionary gravity theory, created in 1916 from a mathematical generalization of his theory of special relativity; it changed our concept of gravity from Newton's universal force to the warping of the geometry of spacetime in the presence of matter and energy.

Geodesic—the shortest path between two neighboring points, which is a straight line in Euclidian geometry, and a unique curved path in four-dimensional spacetime.

Globular cluster—a relatively small, dense system of up to millions of stars occurring commonly in galaxies.

Gravitational lensing—the bending of light by the curvature of spacetime; galaxies and clusters of galaxies act as lenses, distorting the images of distant bright galaxies or quasars as the light passes through or near them.

Gravitational mass—the active mass of a body that produces a gravitational force on other bodies.

Gravitational waves—ripples in the curvature of spacetime predicted by general relativity; although any accelerating body can produce gravitational radiation or waves, those that could be detected by experiments would be caused by cataclysmic cosmic events.

Graviton—the hypothetical smallest packet of gravitational energy, comparable to the photon for electromagnetic energy; the graviton has not yet been seen experimentally.

Group (in mathematics)—in abstract algebra, a set that obeys a binary operation that satisfies certain axioms; for example, the property of addition of integers makes a group; the branch of mathematics that studies groups is called group theory.

Hadron—a generic word for fermion particles that undergo strong nuclear interactions.

Hamiltonian—an alternative way of deriving the differential equations of motion for a physical system using the calculus of variations; Hamilton's principle is also called the "principle of stationary action" and was originally formulated by Sir William Rowan Hamilton for classical mechanics; the principle applies to classical fields such as the gravitational and electromagnetic fields, and has had important applications in quantum mechanics and quantum field theory.

Homogeneous—in cosmology, when the universe appears the same to all observers, no matter where they are in the universe.

Inertia—the tendency of a body to remain in uniform motion once it is moving, and to stay at rest if it is at rest; Galileo discovered the law of inertia in the early seventeenth century.

Inertial mass—the mass of a body that resists an external force; since Newton, it has been known experimentally that inertial and gravitational mass are equal; Einstein used this equivalence of inertial and gravitational mass to postulate his equivalence principle, which was a cornerstone of his gravity theory.

Inflation theory—a theory proposed by Alan Guth and others to resolve the flatness, horizon, and homogeneity problems in the standard big bang model; the very early universe is pictured as expanding exponentially fast in a fraction of a second.

Interferometry—the use of two or more telescopes, which in combination create a receiver in effect as large as the distance between them; radio astronomy in particular makes use of interferometry.

Inverse square law—discovered by Newton, based on earlier work by Kepler, this law states that the force of gravity between two massive bodies or point particles decreases as the inverse square of the distance between them.

Isotropic—in cosmology, when the universe looks the same to an observer, no matter in which direction she looks.

Kelvin temperature scale—designed by Lord Kelvin (William Thomson) in the mid-1800s to measure very cold temperatures, its starting point is absolute zero, the coldest possible temperature in the universe, corresponding to −273.15 degrees Celsius; water's freezing point is 273.15K (0°C), while its boiling point is 373.15K (100°C).

Lagrange points—discovered by the Italian-French mathematician Joseph-Louis Lagrange, these five special points are in the vicinity of two orbiting masses where a third, smaller mass can orbit at a fixed distance from the larger masses; at the Lagrange points, the gravitational pull of the two large masses precisely equals the centripetal force required to keep the third body, such as a satellite, in a bound orbit; three of the Lagrange points are unstable, two are stable.

Lagrangian—named after Joseph-Louis Lagrange, and denoted by L, this mathematical expression summarizes the dynamical properties of a physical system; it is defined in classical mechanics as the kinetic energy T minus the potential energy V; the equations of motion of a system of particles may be derived from the Euler-Lagrange equations, a family of partial differential equations.

Light cone—a mathematical means of expressing past, present, and future space and time in terms of spacetime geometry; in four-dimensional Minkowski spacetime, the light rays emanating from or arriving at an event separate spacetime into a past cone and a future cone which meet at a point corresponding
to the event.

Lorentz transformations—mathematical transformations from one inertial frame of reference to another such that the laws of physics remain the same; named after Hendrik Lorentz, who developed them in 1904, these transformations form the basic mathematical equations underlying special relativity.

Mercury anomaly—a phenomenon in which the perihelion of Mercury's orbit advances more rapidly than predicted by Newton's equations of gravity; when Einstein showed that his gravity theory predicted the anomalous precession, it was the first empirical evidence that general relativity might be correct.

Meson—a short-lived boson composed of a quark and an antiquark, believed to bind protons and neutrons together in the atomic nucleus.

Metric tensor—mathematical symmetric tensor coefficients that determine the infinitesimal distance between two points in spacetime; in effect the metric tensor distinguishes between Euclidean and non-Euclidean geometry.

Michelson-Morley experiment—1887 experiment by Albert Michelson and Edward Morley that proved that the ether did not exist; beams of light traveling in the same direction, and in the perpendicular direction, as the supposed ether showed no difference in speed or arrival time at their destination.

Milky Way—the spiral galaxy that contains our solar system.

Minkowski spacetime—the geometrically flat spacetime, with no gravitational effects, first described by the Swiss mathematician Hermann Minkowski; it became the setting of Einstein's theory of gravity.

MOG—my relativistic modified theory of gravitation, which generalizes Einstein's general relativity; MOG stands for "Modified Gravity."

MOND—a modification of Newtonian gravity published by Mordehai Milgrom in 1983; this is a nonrelativistic phenomenological model used to describe rotational velocity curves of galaxies; MOND stands for "Modified Newtonian Dynamics."

Neutrino—an elementary particle with zero electric charge; very difficult to detect, it is created in radioactive decays and is able to pass through matter almost undisturbed; it is considered to have a tiny mass that has not yet been accurately measured.

Neutron—an elementary and electrically neutral particle found in the atomic nucleus, and having about the same mass as the proton.

Nuclear force—another name for the strong force that binds protons and neutrons together in the atomic nucleus.

Nucleon—a generic name for a proton or neutron within the atomic nucleus.

Neutron star—the collapsed core of a star that remains after a supernova explosion; it is extremely dense, relatively small, and composed of neutrons.

Newton's gravitational constant—the constant of proportionality, G, which occurs in the Newtonian law of gravitation, and says that the attractive force between
two bodies is proportional to the product of their masses and inversely proportional to the square of the distance between them; its numerical value is: $G = 6.67428 \pm 0.00067 \times 10^{-11}$ m3 kg–1 s–2.

Nonsymmetric field theory (Einstein)—a mathematical description of the geometry of spacetime based on a metric tensor that has both a symmetric part and an antisymmetric part; Einstein used this geometry to formulate a unified field theory of gravitation and electromagnetism.

Nonsymmetric Gravitation Theory (NGT)—my generalization of Einstein's purely gravitation theory (general relativity) that introduces the antisymmetric field as an extra component of the gravitational field; mathematically speaking, the nonsymmetric field structure is described by a non-Riemannian geometry.

Parallax—the apparent movement of a nearer object relative to a distant background when one views the object from two different positions; used with triangulation for measuring distances in astronomy.

Paradigm shift—a revolutionary change in belief, popularized by the philosopher Thomas Kuhn, in which the majority of scientists in a given field discard a traditional theory of nature in favor of a new one that passes the tests of experiment and observation; Darwin's theory of natural selection, Newton's gravity theory, and Einstein's general relativity all represented paradigm shifts.

Parsec—a unit of astronomical length equal to 3.262 light years.

Particle-wave duality—the fact that light in all parts of the electromagnetic spectrum (including radio waves, X-rays, etc., as well as visible light) sometimes acts like waves and sometimes acts like particles or photons; gravitation may be similar, manifesting as waves in spacetime or graviton particles.

Perihelion—the position in a planet's elliptical orbit when it is closest to the sun.

Perihelion advance—the movement, or changes, in the position of a planet's perihelion in successive revolutions of its orbit over time; the most dramatic perihelion advance is Mercury's, whose orbit traces a rosette pattern.

Perturbation theory—a mathematical method for finding an approximate solution to an equation that cannot be solved exactly, by expanding the solution in a series in which each successive term is smaller than the preceding one.

Phion—name given to the massive vector field in MOG; it is represented both by a boson particle, which carries the fifth force, and a field.

Photoelectric effect—the ejection of electrons from a metal by X-rays, which proved the existence of photons; Einstein's explanation of this effect in 1905 won him the Nobel Prize in 1921; separate experiments proving and demonstrating
the existence of photons were performed in 1922 by Thomas Millikan and Arthur Compton, who received the Nobel Prize for this work in 1923 and 1927, respectively.

Photon—the quantum particle that carries the energy of electromagnetic waves; the spin of the photon is 1 times Planck's constant h.

Pioneer 10 and 11 spacecraft—launched by NASA in the early 1970s to explore the outer solar system, these spacecraft show a small, anomalous acceleration as they leave the inner solar system.

Planck's constant (h)—a fundamental constant that plays a crucial role in quantum mechanics, determining the size of quantum packages of energy such as the photon; it is named after Max Planck, a founder of quantum mechanics

Principle of general covariance—Einstein's principle that the laws of physics remain the same whatever the frame of reference an observer uses to measure physical quantities.

Principle of least action—more accurately the principle of *stationary* action, this variational principle, when applied to a mechanical system or a field theory, can be used to derive the equations of motion of the system; the credit for discovering the principle is given to Pierre-Louis Moreau Maupertius but it may have been discovered independently by Leonhard Euler or Gottfried Leibniz.

Proton—an elementary particle that carries positive electrical charge and is the nucleus of a hydrogen atom.

Ptolemaic model of the universe—the predominant theory of the universe until the Renaissance, in which the Earth was the heavy center of the universe and all other heavenly bodies, including the moon, sun, planets, and stars, orbited around it; named for Claudius Ptolemy.

Quantize—to apply the principles of quantum mechanics to the behavior of matter and energy (such as the electromagnetic or gravitational field energy); breaking down a field into its smallest units or packets of energy.

Quantum field theory—the modern relativistic version of quantum mechanics used to describe the physics of elementary particles; it can also be used in nonrelativistic fieldlike systems in condensed matter physics.

Quantum gravity—attempts to unify gravity with quantum mechanics.

Quantum mechanics—the theory of the interaction between quanta (radiation) and matter; the effects of quantum mechanics become observable at the submicroscopic distance scales of atomic and particle physics, but macroscopic quantum effects can be seen in the phenomenon of quantum entanglement.

Quantum spin—the intrinsic quantum angular momentum of an elementary particle; this is in contrast to the classical orbital angular momentum of a body rotating about a point in space.

Quark—the fundamental constituent of all particles that interact through the strong nuclear force; quarks are fractionally charged, and come in several varieties; because they are confined within particles such as protons and neutrons, they cannot be detected as free particles.

Quasars—"quasi-stellar objects," the farthest distant objects that can be detected with radio and optical telescopes; they are exceedingly bright, and are believed to be young, newly forming galaxies; it was the discovery of quasars in 1960 that quashed the steady-state theory of the universe in favor of the big bang.

Quintessence—a fifth element in the ancient Greek worldview, along with earth, water, fire and air, whose purpose was to move the crystalline spheres that supported the heavenly bodies orbiting the Earth; eventually this concept became known as the "ether," which provided the *something* that bodies needed to be in contact with in order to move; although Einstein's special theory of relativity dispensed with the ether, recent explanations of the acceleration of the universe call the varying negative pressure vacuum energy "quintessence."

Redshift—a useful phenomenon based on the Doppler principle that can indicate whether and how fast bodies in the universe are receding from an observer's position on Earth; as galaxies move rapidly away from us, the frequency of the wavelength of their light is shifted toward the red end of the electromagnetic
spectrum; the amount of this shifting indicates the distance of the galaxy.

Riemann curvature tensor—a mathematical term that specifies the curvature of four-dimensional spacetime.

Riemannian geometry—a non-Euclidean geometry developed in the mid-nineteenth century by the German mathematician George Bernhard Riemann that describes curved surfaces on which parallel lines *can* converge, diverge, and even intersect, unlike Euclidean geometry; Einstein made

Riemannian geometry the mathematical formalism of general relativity.

Satellite galaxy—a galaxy that orbits a host galaxy or even a cluster of galaxies.

Scalar field—a physical term that associates a value without direction to every point in space, such as temperature, density, and pressure; this is in contrast to a vector field, which has a direction in space; in Newtonian physics or in electrostatics, the potential energy is a scalar field and its gradient is the vector force field; in quantum field theory, a scalar field describes a boson particle with spin zero.

Scale invariance—distribution of objects or patterns such that the same shapes and distributions remain if one increases or decreases the size of the length scales or space in which the objects are observed; a common example of scale invariance is fractal patterns.

Schwarzschild solution—an exact spherically symmetric static solution of Einstein's field equations in general relativity, worked out by the astronomer Karl Schwarzschild in 1916, which predicted the existence of black holes.

Self-gravitating system—a group of objects or astrophysical bodies held together by mutual gravitation, such as a cluster of galaxies; this is in contrast to a "bound system" like our solar system, in which bodies are mainly attracted to and revolve around a central mass.

Singularity—a place where the solutions of differential equations break down; a spacetime singularity is a position in space where quantities used to determine the gravitational field become infinite; such quantities include the curvature of spacetime and the density of matter.

Spacetime—in relativity theory, a combination of the three dimensions of space with time into a four-dimensional geometry; first introduced into relativity by Hermann Minkowski in 1908.

Special theory of relativity—Einstein's initial theory of relativity, published in 1905, in which he explored the "special" case of transforming the laws of physics from one uniformly moving frame of reference to another; the equations of special relativity revealed that the speed of light is a constant, that objects appear contracted in the direction of motion when moving at close to the speed of light, and that E = mc2, or energy is equal to mass times the speed of light squared.

Spin—see quantum spin.

String theory—a theory based on the idea that the smallest units of matter are not point particles but vibrating strings; a popular research pursuit in physics for two decades, string theory has some attractive mathematical features, but has yet to make a testable prediction.

Strong force—see nuclear force.

Supernova—spectacular, brilliant death of a star by explosion and the release of heavy elements into space; supernovae type 1a are assumed to have the same intrinsic brightness and are therefore used as standard candles in estimating cosmic distances.

Supersymmetry—a theory developed in the 1970s which, proponents claim, describes the most fundamental spacetime symmetry of particle physics: For every boson particle there is a supersymmetric fermion partner, and for every fermion there exists a supersymmetric boson partner; to date, no supersymmetric particle partner has been detected.

Tully-Fisher law—a relation stating that the asymptotically flat rotational velocity of a star in a galaxy, raised to the fourth power, is proportional to the mass or luminosity of the galaxy.

Unified theory (or unified field theory)—a theory that unites the forces of nature; in Einstein's day those forces consisted of electromagnetism and gravity; today the weak and strong nuclear forces must also be taken into account, and perhaps someday MOG's fifth force or skew force will be included; no one has yet discovered a successful unified theory.

Vacuum—in quantum mechanics, the lowest energy state, which corresponds to the vacuum state of particle physics; the vacuum in modern quantum field theory is the state of perfect balance of creation and annihilation of particles and antiparticles.

Variable Speed of Light (VSL) cosmology—an alternative to inflation theory, in which the speed of light was much faster at the beginning of the universe than it is today; like inflation, this theory solves the horizon and flatness problems in the very early universe in the standard big bang model.

Vector field—a physical value that assigns a field with the position and direction of a vector in space; it describes the force field of gravity or the electric and magnetic force fields in James Clerk Maxwell's field equations.

Virial theorem—a means of estimating the average speed of galaxies within galaxy clusters from their estimated average kinetic and potential energies.

Vulcan—a hypothetical planet predicted by the nineteenth-century astronomer Urbain Jean Joseph Le Verrier to be the closest orbiting planet to the sun; the presence of Vulcan would explain the anomalous precession of the perihelion of Mercury's orbit; Einstein later explained the anomalous precession in general relativity by gravity alone.

Weak force—one of the four fundamental forces of nature, associated with radioactivity such as beta decay in subatomic physics; it is much weaker than the strong nuclear force but still much stronger than gravity.

X-ray clusters—galaxy clusters with large amounts of extremely hot gas within them that emit X-rays; in such clusters, this hot gas represents at least twice the mass of the luminous stars.

Bibliography

Balungi Francis, (2010) "A hypothetical investigation into the realm of the microscopic and macroscopic universes beyond the standard model" general physics arXiv:1002.2287v1 [physics.gen-ph]

Hawking, Stephen (1975). "Particle Creation by Black Holes". Commun. Math. Phys. 43 (3): 199–220. Bibcode:1975CMaPh..43..199H.

Hawking, S. W. (1974). "Black hole explosions?". Nature.248(5443):30–31. Bibcode:1974Natur.248...30H.doi:10.1038/248030a0.

Carlo Rovelli (2003) "Quantum Gravity" Draft of the Book Pdf Some few texts used are from Wikipedia https://creativecommons.org/licenses/by-sa/3.0/
D. N. Page, Phys. Rev. D 13, 198 (1976).

C. Gao and Y.Lu, Pulsations of a black hole in LQG (2012) arXiv:1706.08009v3
A.H. Chamseddine and V.Mukhanov, Non singular black hole (2016) arXiv 1612.05861v1

M.Bojowald and G.M.Paily, A no-singularity scenario in LQG (2012) arXiv: 1206.5765v1

P.Singh, class.Quant.Grav,26,125005(2009), arXiv:0901.2750

P.Singh and F.Vidotto, Phys.Rev, D83,064027(2011) arXiv:1012.1307

C.Rovelli and F.Vidotto, Phy. Rev,111(9) 091303(2013) arXiv:1307.3228v2

M.Bojowald, Initial conditions for a universe, Gravity Research Foundation (2003)

A.Ashtekar, Singularity Resolution in Loop Quantum Cosmology (2008) arXiv:0812.4703v1

J.Brunneumann and T.Thiemann, On singularity avoidance in Loop Quantum Gravity (2005) arXiv:0505032v1

L.Modesto, Disappearence of the Black hole singularity in Quantum gravity (2004) arXiv:0407097v2

Mikhailov, A.A. (1959).Mon. Not. Roy. Astron. Soc.,119, 593.

P. Merat etal.(1974). Astron & Astrophys 32, 471-475

Trempler, R.J. (1956).Helv. Phys. Acta, Suppl.,IV, 106.

Trempler, R.J. (1932). " The deflection of light in the sun's gravitational field "Astronomical society of the pacific 167

Einstein, A. (1916).Ann. d. Phys.,49, 769; (1923).The Principle of Relativity, (translators Perret, W. and Jeffery, G.B.), (Dover Publications, Inc., New York), pp. 109–164.

Von Klüber, H. (1960). InVistas in Astronomy, Vol. 3, pp. 47–77.

K. Hentschel (1992). Erwin Finlay Freundlich and testing Einstein theory of relativity, Communicated by J.D. North
Muhleman, D.O., Ekers, R.D. and Fomalont, E.B. (1970).Phys. Rev. Lett.,24, 1377

Mikhailov, A.A. (1956).Astron. Zh.,33, 912.

Dyson, F.W., Eddington, A.S. and Davidson, C. (1920).Phil. Trans. Roy. sog., A220, 291

Chant, C.A. and Young, R.K. (1924).Publ. Dom. Astron. Obs.,2, 275.

Campbell, W.W. and Trumbler, R.J. (1923).Lick Obs. Bull.,11, 41.

Freundlich, E.F., von Klüber, H. and von Brunn, A. (1931).Abhandl. Preuss. Akad. Wiss. Berlin, Phys. Math. Kl., No.l;Z. Astrophys.,3, 171

Mikhailov, A.A. (1949).Expeditions to Observe the Total Solar Eclipse of 21 September, 1941, (report), (ed. Fesenkov, V.G.), (Publications of the Academy of Sciences, U.S.S.R.), pp. 337–351.

S.P. Martin, in Perspectives on Supersymmetry , edited by G.L. Kane (World Scientific, Singapore, 1998) pp. 1–98; and a longer archive version in hep-ph/9709356; I.J.R. Aitchison, hep-ph/0505105.

Mara Beller, Quantum Dialogue: The Making of a Revolution. University of Chicago Press, Chicago, 2001.

Morrison, Philp: "The Neutrino, scientific American, Vol 194,no.1 (1956),pp.58-68.
R. Haag, J. T. Lopuszanski and M. Sohnius, Nucl. Phys. B88, 257 (1975) S.R. Coleman and J. Mandula, Phys.Rev. 159 (1967) 1251.

H.P. Nilles, Phys. Reports 110, 1 (1984).

P. Nath, R. Arnowitt, and A.H. Chamseddine, Applied $N = 1$ Supergravity (World Scientific, Singapore, 1984).

S.P. Martin, in Perspectives on Supersymmetry , edited by G.L. Kane (World Scientific, Singapore, 1998) pp. 1–98; and a longer archive version in hep-ph/9709356; I.J.R. Aitchison, hep-ph/0505105.

S. Weinberg, The Quantum Theory of Fields, VolumeIII: Supersymmetry (Cambridge University Press, Cambridge,UK, 2000).

E. Witten, Nucl. Phys. B188, 513 (1981).

S. Dimopoulos and H. Georgi, Nucl. Phys. B193, 150(1981).

N. Sakai, Z. Phys. C11, 153 (1981);R.K. Kaul, Phys. Lett. 109B, 19 (1982).

L. Susskind, Phys. Reports 104, 181 (1984).
L. Girardello and M. Grisaru, Nucl. Phys. B194, 65(1982); L.J. Hall and L. Randall,

Phys. Rev. Lett. 65, 2939(1990);I. Jack and D.R.T. Jones, Phys. Lett. B457, 101 (1999).

For a review, see N. Polonsky, Supersymmetry: Structureand phenomena. Extensions of the standard model, Lect.Notes Phys. M68, 1 (2001).

G. Bertone, D. Hooper and J. Silk, Phys. Reports 405, 279 (2005).

G. Jungman, M. Kamionkowski, and K. Griest, Phys. Reports 267, 195 (1996).

V. Agrawal, S.M. Barr, J.F. Donoghue and D. Seckel,Phys. Rev. D57, 5480 (1998).

N. Arkani-Hamed and S. Dimopoulos, JHEP 0506, 073(2005); G.F. Giudice and A. Romanino, Nucl. Phys. B699, 65(2004) [erratum: B706, 65 (2005)]. July 27, 2006 11:28

en.wikipedia.org/wiki/Supersymmetry - 52k - Cached - Similar pages en.wikipedia.org/wiki/Grand_unification_theory - 39k - Cached - Similar pages

In cosmology, the Planck epoch (or Planck era), named after Max Planck, is the earliest period of time in the history of the universe, en.wikipedia.org/wiki/**Planck_epoch** - 23k - Cached - Similar pages

L. Shapiro and J. Sol`a, Phys. Lett. B 530, 10 (2002);

E. V.Gorbar and I. L. Shapiro, JHEP 02, 021 (2003); A. M. Pelinson,

L. Shapiro, and F. I. Takakura, Nucl. Phys. B 648, 417 (2003).

A. Starobinsky, Phys. Lett. B 91, 99 (1980).

G. F. R. Ellis, J. Murugan, and C. G. Tsagas, Class. Quant. Grav.21, 233 (2004).

H. V. Peiris et al., Astrophys. J. Suppl. 148, 213 (2003).

D. N. Spergel et al., astro-ph/0603449.

Vilenkin, Phys. Rev. D 32, 2511 (1985).

A. Starobinsky, Pis'ma Astron. Zh 9, 579 (1983).

A.H. Guth, Phys. Rev. D23, 347 (1981).

A.D. Linde, Phys. Lett. B108, 389 (1982); A. Albrecht, P.J. Steinhardt, Phys.Rev. Lett. 48, 1220 (1982).

A.D. Linde, Phys Lett. B129, 177 (1983).

N. Makino, M. Sasaki, Prog. Theor. Phys. 86, 103 (1991);

D. Kaiser, Phys. Rev.D52, 4295 (1995).

H. Goldberg, Phys. Rev. Lett. 50, 1419 (1983).

E. Kolb and M. Turner, The Early Universe (Addison-Wesley, Reading, MA,1990).

W. Garretson and E. Carlson, Phys. Lett. B 315, 232(1993); H. Goldberg, hep-ph/0003197.

Eddington, A. S., The Internal Constitution of the Stars (Cambridge University Press, England,1926), p. 16

Duncan R .C. & Thompson C., Ap.J.392, L 9 (1992).
Thompson , C, Duncan , R .C ., Woods , P., Kouveliotou , C ., Finger , M.H. & van Parad ij s , J .,ApJ, submitted , astro-ph /9908086, (2000).

Schwinger , J .,Phys. Rev.73, 416L (1948)

Carlip, S.: Quantum gravity: a progress report. Rept. Prog. Phys. 64, 885 (2001).arXiv:gr-qc/0108040

Kerr,R.P.: Gravitational field of a spinning mass as an example of algebraically special metrics.

Phys. Rev. Lett. 11, 237–238 (1963)

Bekenstein, J.: Black holes and the second law. Lett. Nuovo Cim. 4, 737–740 (1972)

Bardeen, J.M., Carter, B., Hawking, S.: The four laws of black hole mechanics. Commun.

Math. Phys. 31, 161–170 (1973)

Tolman, R.: Relativity, Thermodynamics, and Cosmology. Dover Books on Physics Series.

Dover Publications, New York (1987)

Oppenheimer, J., Volkoff, G.: On massive neutron cores. Phys. Rev. 55, 374–381 (1939)

Tolman, R.C.: Static solutions of einstein's field equations for spheres of fluid, Phys. Rev. 55,364–373 (1939)

Zel'dovich Y.B.: Zh. Eksp. Teoret. Fiz.41, 1609 (1961)

Bondi, H.: Massive spheres in general relativity. Proc. Roy. Soc. Lond. A281, 303–317 (1964)

Sorkin, R.D., Wald, R.M., Zhang, Z.J.: Entropy of selfgravitating radiation. Gen. Rel. Grav. 1127–1146 (1981)

Newman, E.T., Couch, R., Chinnapared, K., Exton, A., Prakash, A., et al.: Metric of a rotating,charged mass. J. Math. Phys. 6, 918–919 (1965)

Ginzburg, V., Ozernoi, L.: Sov. Phys. JETP 20, 689 (1965)

Doroshkevich, A., Zel'dovich, Y., Novikov I.: Gravitational collapse of nonsymmetric and rotating masses, JETP 49 (1965)

Israel, W.: Event horizons in static vacuum space-times. Phys. Rev. 164, 1776–1779 (1967)

Israel,W.: Event horizons in static electrovac space-times. Commun. Math. Phys. 8, 245–260 (1968)

Loop quantum gravity does provide such a prediction [363, 364], and it disagrees with the semiclassical

Carter, B.: Axisymmetric black hole has only two degrees of freedom. Phys. Rev. Lett. 26, 331–333(1971)

Penrose, R.: Gravitational collapse: the role of general relativity. Riv. Nuovo Cim. 1, 252–276 (1969)

Christodoulou, D.: Reversible and irreversible transformations in black hole physics. Phys. Rev. Lett. 25, 1596–1597 (1970)

Christodoulou, D., Ruffini, R.: Reversible transformations of a charged black hole. Phys. Rev. D4, 3552–3555 (1971)

Hawking, S.: Particle creation by black holes. Commun. Math. Phys. 43, 199–220 (1975)

Klein, O.: Die reflexion von elektronen an einem potential sprung nach der relativistischen dynamik von dirac. Z. Phys. 53, 157 (1929)

Wald, R.M.: General Relativity. The University of Chicago Press, Chicago (1984)

Hawking, S.W.: Black hole explosions. Nature 248, 30–31 (1974)

Hawking, S., Ellis, G.: The large scale structure of space-time. Cambridge University Press, Cambridge (1973)

Carter, B.: Black hole equilibrium states, In Black Holes—Les astres occlus. Gordon and Breach Science Publishers, (1973)

Hawking, S.W.: Gravitational radiation from colliding black holes. Phys. Rev. Lett. 26, 1344– 1346 (1971)

Hawking, S.: Black holes in general relativity. Commun. Math. Phys. 25, 152–166 (1972)

Bekenstein, J.: Extraction of energy and charge from a black hole. Phys. Rev. D7, 949–953 (1973)

Bekenstein, J.D.: Black holes and entropy. Phys. Rev. D7, 2333–2346 (1973)

Hawking, S.: Quantum gravity and path integrals. Phys. Rev. D18, 1747–1753 (1978)

Gross, D.J., Perry, M.J., Yaffe, L.G.: Instability of flat space at finite temperature. Phys. Rev. D25, 330–355 (1982)

Unruh, W.G., Wald, R.M.: What happens when an accelerating observer detects a rindler particle. Phys. Rev. D29, 1047–1056 (1984)

Bekenstein, J.D.: Auniversal upper bound on the entropy to energy ratio for bounded systems. Phys. Rev. D23, 287 (1981)

Unruh,W.,Wald, R.M.: Acceleration radiation and generalized second law of thermodynamics. Phys. Rev. D25, 942–958 (1982)

Unruh, W., Wald, R.M.: Entropy bounds, acceleration radiation, and the generalized second law. Phys. Rev. D27, 2271–2276 (1983)

Image : MPI for gravitational physics / W.Benger-zib

Tomilin,K.A., (1999). "Natural Systems Of Units: To The Centenary Aniniversary Of   The Planck Systems", 287-296

Sivaram, C. (2007). "What Is Special About the Planck Mass"? arXiv:0707.0058v1

H. Georgi and S.L. Glahow. (1974) "Unity Of All Elementary-Particle Forces". Phys. Rev. Letters 32, 438

Luigi Maxmilian Caligiuri, Amrit Sorli. Gravity Originates from Variable Energy Density of Quantum Vacuum. American Journal of Modern Physics. Vol. 3, No. 3, 2014, pp. 118-128. doi: 10.11648/j.ajmp.20140303.11

Philip J. Tattersall,(2018) Quantum Vacuum Energy and the Emergence of Gravity. doi:10.5539/apr.v10n2p1

H. E. Puthoff (1989) Gravity as a zero-point-fluctuation force PHYSICAL REVIEW A VOLUME 39, NUMBER 5

Balungi Francis (2018) "Quantum Gravity in a Nutshell1" Book.

E.Verlinde (2016) Emergent Gravity and the Dark Universe, arXiv:1611.02269v2[hep-th]

S.Hossenfelder (2018) The Redshift-Dependence of Radial Acceleration: Modified gravity versus particle dark matter, arXiv:1803.08683v1[gr-qc]

Robert J. Scherrer (2004) Purely kinetic k-essence as unified dark matter, arXiv:astro-ph/0402316v3

J.S.Farnes (2018), Aunifying theory of dark energy and dark matter: Negative masses and matter creation within a modified ΛCDM framework, arXiv:1712.07962v2[physics.gen-ph]

Gustav M Obermair (2013), Primordial Planck mass black holes (PPMBHs) as candidates for dark matter? J. Phys:conf.Ser.442012066

V.Cooray etal...(2017), An alternative approach to estimate the vacuum energy density of free space, doi:10.20944/preprints201707.0048.v1

M.Milgrom, (1983) A modification of the Newtonian dynamics: Implications for galaxies, Astrophys.J.270, 371.

Acknowledgments

This book would never have been completed without the patience and dedication of my wife, Wanyana Ritah. She performed the wonderful and difficult task of editing major parts of the book and helped in researching many details necessary to complete it.

I wish to thank several colleagues for their help and extensive comments on the manuscript, including Lee Smolin, Carlo Rovelli, Sabine Hossenfelder, Jim Baggot and Viktor Toth. I also thank my colleagues Harvey Brown, Paul Frampton, Stacy McGaugh, and Lee Smolin for helpful comments. I particularly thank a total of 200 online physics friends and SUSP science foundation members, for a careful reading of the manuscript. Many graduate students have contributed over the years to developing my Quantum theory of gravity.

I also wish to thank my editors, at SUSP science Foundation for their enthusiasm and support. Finally, I thank our family for their patience, love, and support during the four years of working on this book.

Lightning Source UK Ltd.
Milton Keynes UK
UKHW010204070220
358308UK00001B/43/J